HEALING WHILE HURTING

Carolina Ayala

Copyright © 2020 by Carolina Ayala-Velasquez

Created and self-published by Carolina Ayala-Velasquez

Cover by Edgardo Velasquez and Carolina Ayala-Velasquez

Illustrations by Angel, Iris and Leonardo

All rights reserved.

No part of this book may be used or reprinted in any way without expressed written permission from the author and artists.

Healing while Hurting/ Carolina M-G Ayala. —1st ed.

ISBN 978-1-953449-14-6

Printed in the United States of America

Contents

Dedication..1
Introduction..5
Healing while hurting
(the first days, weeks, months, years)..........................13
Thankful (what helped and helps me through)
(how I/we honor you)..232
Grateful (what I've learned/wish I knew).......................238
Blessed (thank you, about me)......................................241

This book is in honor of my dad, to celebrate his life and to appreciate him always even after his passing. This book is dedicated to my children Angel, Iris, Leonardo and Athena. I know you miss your grandpa so much everyday and I hope you always know he is watching over you. I hope this book helps keep memories alive, love alive , hope alive and healing happening.

I hope this can remind you that it is ok to not be ok. I also want you to know that it is ok to be ok. At times both of these very different feelings-can feel wrong. Whatever it is you are feeling is never wrong and I love you very much.

To all of our family, to everyone who has been affected by this loss or any other loss-this is for you and I hope it serves a purpose beyond my own healing journey.

Now

Not getting lost in how
I just know. that I know now.
Now is the time,
the time to shine.
and I feel it within every part of me,
this is the next part for me.
It doesn't matter how it will get done,
but I can see it, I can feel it, I know that it will get done.
it's been a part of me so long,
the hardest parts I have overcome.
the work is always being done and now to complete this piece for peace,
now to heal and fulfill this destined part of me.
as I start to put the pieces together more,
the tears fall and I am more for sure.
I am so ready for this next course,
and still it will only be the beginning, because this can never be over.
dad, you are on my mind. heavy on my heart,
you continue to help me through, from finish to start.
from beginning to end
and to start over again.
love you, always and forever
forever and always
   8/21/20

Introduction to a piece of the journey

Our life had changed many times before the day my dad left this earth. We have had many transformative dates in our lives individually and our life together. The day I learned my father had cancer was one of them. Every time he survived and recovered from a radiation or operation or hospital visit was always life changing. The last few months of him and I living together was a whole new layer to this journey and it was also the beginning to the end. The first year without him was a process in itself. The first days, weeks, months-every moment was a part of this journey of healing. All of the days and months and years after that. Each birthday and holiday. It felt and still feels like every moment is a new ending and beginning. Every step is a new step on this path of healing. Every experience brings me closer to him and closer to me.

As you continue to go on this journey with me by reading this book, I think you may feel as if you are reading my diary. These writings and reflections come straight from my journals and Facebook posts-as they were written.

As I was going through things, I often didn't care about grammar and punctuation and anything else-except for the message I needed to get out so that I could continue moving forward.

What you will find in this book is not everything this journey has taken me through. It is just some of the pieces that I hope in putting together can help me and others on this road of grief and healing.

I Remember

I remember the day you told me you had cancer,
You came with other family members.
You didn't want to do this on your own,
You knew you needed support and that I would need it too.

I remember acting like I knew
I was supposed to be your go to.
We didn't keep secrets
I felt hurt for many reasons.

I know why you took your time to tell me
You knew once I knew, it'd be reality.
You didn't want me to treat you differently
You didn't want to be the one to hurt me.

I remember being so angry
I asked GOD "why are you doing this to me?"
I pleaded with God to heal you
That nothing in your past could deserve such a painful truth.
I tried to reason with what was going on
I tried to make sense of what I felt was so wrong.
I remember saying and believing in recovery
I started doing research to back up my beliefs and feelings.

You wanted to be treated like nothing was wrong
I wanted to feel that too, so for so long I went along

You shared the truth because you didn't want secrets-it was too much to carry
I remember hugging you that day, felt so differently
But I didn't want you to feel different around me
I knew life would forever be changed for you and for me.

I didn't live with you
I didn't see just how much you went through
I didn't want to
You didn't want me to.

I remember I cried so much
I remember, you felt like you told me too much
I remember asking you to allow me to feel
I needed to feel it all so that I could learn to deal,
Many days I didn't want to accept what was real
Many days I told myself to prepare for not being able to heal.

9/5/20

Immediately

The day I found out you had cancer I cried so much
You never wanted to tell me too much.
Trying to protect me from pain
And in the same breathe I just wanted to do the same.
I wanted to protect you
I wanted to save you.
I made it clear from day one
It hurts the most to not know, to find out later from someone.
I started to research, call doctors
I came across the hope of living donor.
I immediately told you
I would give half of my liver to you.
I'd do it in a heartbeat no questions asked
I'd do it in a second with no regrets.
You had hope saying it'd be a new life
Your eyes dimmed saying you can't risk anyone else's life.
You said this is your life, your faith was in a higher power
You wanted to let this journey run its natural course no matter whatever.
Cancer gave you fear, sadness, pain
You never showed anything besides a smile on your face.
I just wanted to save you

I thought I was the perfect one too.
Your only child, your blood
I've never done any type of "drug."
I thought I'd be the perfect match
But our blood type just wasn't a match.
How crazy is that?
I just want you back.
With every chemotherapy you were scared you wouldn't wake up
With every situation you just wanted to see me when you looked up.
You called me your angel
Now you are mine
I love you dad.

10/21/14

In November you fainted and had to be rushed to the hospital. You spent many days there recovering, missing thanksgiving. I still made thanksgiving happen the day you were released. Not only that but I had you moved out of your house and set up here in the kids' room to be close to us so we could watch and help you. I helped you get dressed, stand up, eat, I hugged you when you couldn't stop shaking, tucked you in, made sure throughout the night you were ok, put night lights throughout the house for you to see, kept your phone paid, cable on your tv and anything you asked for.

You told me" I never thought my baby would be taking care of me" I laughed and said always. I'd do it all and more for even longer if I could.

We had this conversation weeks ago. You told me" if a machine is ever what's keeping me alive, you be strong and let me go" I was very honest in saying I could never be that strong but that I will respect your heart and wishes. We both cried and held each other that conversation and then continued living life until that conversation became our reality today. I love you always and forever dad.

1/21/14

Healing while hurting (time stands still while moving on)

I have experienced painful loss before. The passing of my aunt Denise, the passing of my great friend Jossie Adame who called me "little sis", the passing of my cousin Wayne Blocker, the passing of Gilbert Fernandez, The passing of my grandfather Robert Padilla and other relatives that I was too young to really remember moments with (my grandma madeleine, my aunty Pauline, my uncle Larry, my grand-mother Lupe Padilla)

I knew pain before, it hurts like no other.

I knew healing before (healing that never truly heals fully.)

The passing of my dad was the first death that took me on the most painful, life changing journey of all. Each passing has affected me differently, each life matters to me.

January 21, 2014
Today at 12:40pm my dad made his choice to move on to heaven. I cannot express how much I wanted to keep him holding on in the intensive care unit fighting for life. I can't express enough that this was also the right thing to do. My dad told me weeks ago if a machine is what's

keeping him alive then I have to be strong and let him go. That day, we both cried. Today he requested to be surrounded with loved ones to end his battle with liver cancer. The doctors have all said how surprised they are to see someone in his case make it so far. He never complained. He spent money like he was rich. He was there for people when he needed people there for him. He always smiled. His grandchildren kept him alive and happy. I can't believe he's gone. It feels like a bad dream but I am at peace knowing he is at peace. As much as it hurts to have him not home with me, as much as I continue to cry-I know this is what he wanted. This is what he felt was best. I have no choice but to take peace and comfort in that. My dad has so many loved ones, thank you for the support and love and everything. My life will never be the same without him. I will forever be thankful GOD let me have him this long and let us live the life we did. I am forever grateful that GOD gave us the opportunity to be with him to help him over to the other side. I know that everything has been a blessing, even the situations I don't understand.

To my dad:
I love you. Forever and always. Always and forever.
You can never leave us. You will forever live on.

I just can't believe you are gone.
I love you, why can't that be enough to keep us strong?
I still don't want to say goodbye,
we had the chance and we chose not to (who wants to say a final goodbye?)
We shed tears,
I wiped your tears.
We said I love you,
I heard you, so how is it that I can no longer hear you?
We took pictures
But its not the kind you would picture.
These final pictures aren't ones that are of happy times
These photos are more of me trying to hold on to your life.
and we breathed together until you chose to let go
Except I keep breathing while putting everything on hold.
I know you are not gone
And I know you are not here

Can you heal while hurting?
Is this time standing still while its clearly moving on?

Day 1 after

Waking up in tears, no surprise
The past couple months you would wake up to us getting ready for work and school and you would beg to drive. You didn't want any of us to walk and I'd beg you to relax you would always ask for a fried egg with something for breakfast.
you'd thank me so much for everything
and I'd keep telling you there's no need to thank me.
I am your daughter, I love you
When you love some one these are the small things one might do.
we loved each other the same and it was so understood and yet I find myself unable to understand why healing just can't be good.

I'm missing you so much with every detail surrounding me waiting for a sign, that you are here with me.
I know you have many loved ones to visit
I just miss you so much and I want to be selfish.
I feel like writing you on Facebook -somehow, you'll see it
Like somehow you will read it.
Like you will…. respond
I love you and I miss you dad- how is this already day one?

You continue to take care of me

Dad how amazing are you? You continue to do even in heaven.
While planning this very stressful hard moment in my life- you continue to give more than you have already given.
The past 6 hours I have been deciding things
What kind flowers. What kind of casket. Where do I want you to be buried?
Do we want a limo to drive us both days?
Do we want a police escort to help clear the way?
Which chapel? Which church?
Will there be a reception? what prayer cards to support?
So many questions, so much happening so fast
I want this done quick and at the same time I want time to process all of it.
While all of this is happening, I find out great news
You had life insurance saved for me and you.
Dad you knew I'd do it all for you
You knew this would be expensive and that I wouldn't be able to.
In the end you did it all by preparing financially
not just for yourself but for me.
your only daughter, your only child
you knew I'd struggle to make it work but you wanted me to somehow smile.

you knew I'd make it happen but you gave me some peace
life insurance allows me to take the time to grieve.
Life insurance allows me to panic less
Life insure took away so much extra stress.
No one should have to worry about money while dealing with grief
No one should have to worry about honoring their loved ones properly.
I love you.
You continue to amaze and inspire me.

1/22/14

Day 2 after

going through my billions of photos and I can't be happier dad
you always smiled-no one would ever know the pain you
suffered.
no one would ever know the battle you fought because
you did it with a smile and without any complaints
you kept up your energy even when you felt faint.
you helped others until your last moment here
you held on to faith instead of holding on to the fear.
going through all these photos trying to get your
slideshow together
I am so thankful for our moments, for your smile, for
your face, for our pictures.
We had such a good life
I am thankful for you all of the time.
You are my mirror, my motivation, my inspiration
I can't thank GOD enough for making you my dad-you
were the perfect selection.
I can't thank GOD enough for keeping you around for me
Thankful, grateful and blessed- for eternity.
You passed away so young
but some people don't get their dad this long.
I am so thankful because we were so happy
and these memories will be my treasure forever, they will
heal me even as they hurt me.

You

you were here and you were already an angel, you already had wings
you will always be my hero and role model of what strength and love means.
you were always the best dad no matter your occupation or way of life
I always thought highly of you, I was always proud of you.
I wish you saw yourself through my eyes.
you always looked out for everyone
you didn't give up on anyone.
you changed your whole life for me, for us to build a better relationship
you changed your life and GOD let you stick around for my wedding, graduations, and your grandchildren.
GOD kept you here
although fighting cancer was a struggle while staying here.
GOD gave you strength to smile and see life in another way even through all the challenges-you chose to fight and stay.
We made the most of life before we knew you were sick
we have always made the most of life every time, time was spent.
dad I love you, I can't say it enough.
my guardian angel always, but now from above.

I will always wish you were here
I am so thankful for the memories we made while you were here.
I am so happy you are not in any more pain
The pain I did whiteness drove me insane.
dad i love you. Thank you for loving me
day two without you here, I am really struggling.

1/23/14

My wallet

I wish my wallet matched my heart
You deserve the best celebration of life as you depart.
I know you never wanted a lot
I am going to give you all I've got.
I know you know me all too well
to know that I am going to do my very best to give you the very best farewell.
I am just like you,
always trying to do it big without trying to.
it just happens that way huh?
I promise, I know that say don't make promises.
I promise that Wednesday and Thursday you will be so happy and proud of me like you always have been
I am going to do all I can with the money I have, the support I have and the insurance you've given.
I promise you that you would love how this all turns out
Honoring and celebrating you is what it's all about.
I promise you that it didn't end January 21, 2014 when you went to sleep and went to heaven
That was just an ending to a new beginning in the kingdom of peace and happiness.
I promise you that your life celebration doesn't end next week

We will always cherish you with more than just memories.
you are a piece of me, my heart, my children and everyone who knew you
I am not alone in the feelings I am feeling about you.
I love you so much
thank you for being my dad-for showing me what a real genuine soul is.

Win, win -situation

you always told me and everyone that you were in a win win situation
you said when you are here you are winning and when you go, you'll be winning in heaven.
you always told me to be strong, while we cried
you always told me you were proud and loved me, you wanted to say it while you were alive.
you always told me as long as you are here, you'll do anything for me
disabled but still able, was your saying.
you would do anything for anyone even while you were hurting
and I think doing so much for others is what kept you at ease, it kept you going.
you were just being you doing what you loved to do
you loved those you loved, you had love for strangers too.
we talked about so much, and in a time like this you'd be the first one I call for support
but now you aren't here to call on the phone, I have to close my eyes and pray and hope to hear your words.
I have your phone, your wallet, your clothes and belongings
it's just so hard to believe that this is all real and that this pain is somehow healing.

Healing While Hurting

I always knew the time would come and I always knew it would be hard
but it's harder than I ever could have imagined, you can't prepare for this part.
I am so thankful for your strength, your time here and the memories
Healing while hurting will now be what serves me.

Your final outfit

I tried to pick out your last outfit today. I couldn't do it alone
With the help of grandma Katie, Elise and Juan it has been done.
I originally thought raiders but then going through your clothes
you have such a nice style so I think we found perfection easily when we stopped to think of you.
it's so hard for me
the smell of you, the image, this room, all your belongings.
I miss you so much, it just doesn't feel real at all
I wish you could come back to me, please help me through it all.
You told me before you don't like suits, not even at my wedding
But of course, you loved it that day, you loved it for me.
The past couple of months it was slippers, sweats and robes
but for your last day it will be all style; with your button up, dickies, scarf and all.
It's going to be perfect
I know it.
I just hope I can do this

every day is full of new reality, New sadness.
Every day is full of New struggles and new challenges
but I'm getting it done one step at a time and I have love
to guide me through this.

as Wednesday is getting closer it feels harder to breathe
I'm not going to want to leave your side, even if the sight
is a hard one to see.
I'm not going to be able handle seeing you there
looking different-not being able to wake you, this doesn't
feel fair.
hearing your music, seeing your pictures
Family and friends all at once, its all too much to picture.
dad please help me through this
trying to picture it all isn't helpful but I can't stop myself
from doing it.
Picking up the banner had me in tears
picked up the in-memory cards and I couldn't stop the tears.
The cashier said " I had no idea he was sick. He's so
young and happy"
I was in tears again, came home to see my aunty.
Aunty Leila and Jenny, your sisters
talking with them I could feel you here.
Talking with them felt as though you were just away
Like when you lived in Fremont and you were just a
drive away.

They left and I couldn't stop crying again
missing you home dad wishing you were here and all of this was different.
I just want you here
I am literally having to live out and face this fear.
it's so hard to relive this past week
and know we still have this week of pain and struggle to get through, has me kind of weak.
I am not defeated
How am I going to do this?
I don't know how I am going to hold it together
I also know I do not have to- is this process forever?

1/23/14

Day 3 after

Going through all your fb posts realizing I had to say
"hope you get better" way too many times
I said I miss you so much, we both never liked to say
goodbye.
noticing how much pain you were in
feeling some regret of not being there the way I have been.
I see some pictures of you smiling like the happiest man
on earth
some of those days you were so hurt.
It hurt you to walk, you had stomach pain
you didn't feel good but you didn't complain.
No one would be able to ever know that unless they knew
sometimes I knew but you still smiled, just so I could
smile too.
you still kept going as if nothing was wrong
we knew your situation for years and we never let that
change us.
You never let cancer stop us, cripple us or stop plans
we did so much we both wanted to see happen.
we had some things we never made it to do
(Washington trip, fishing, pedicure, Reno, Tahoe, family
pictures too.)
looking back at all the love, the places we went

the moments we shared, the happiness that took place over the phone calls, fb, texts and visits.
Having you live with me the last couple of months meant the world
to not only you but it meant everything to me and the kids couldn't have been happier.
we got to breathe a little easier, smile a lot more
not have to say bye, just goodnight and see you later.
You living with us meant we got to enjoy time without many interruptions
It meant all new experiences.

Anticipating next week

I must be honest when I say I am scared to face next
Wednesday and Thursday
I wish time would slow down but at the same time I
want you to your resting place.
I went and made arrangements the day after you passed
because I couldn't stand leaving you in that hospital
room, alone -not knowing where you were at.
I can't stand the thought of leaving you-not having you
in your final resting spot
I want to make sure your dressed, warm and comfortable.
I want you with us again
I am so scared to see you looking different.
I am so scared to have to leave you again
I am so scared of how I am going to handle this.
You've always known my love is so strong that my tears
won't break me
for you I will to be strong and smile because I know you
don't want me ever crying.
I know you never want to see me sad
Understand this is me healing dad.
Understand these tears are a sign of my love
I will celebrate that smile you have and pass it on.
You passed down your smile, love, positivity and faith
Everyone you have met is forever blessed with these traits.

Tears fall so easily, my appetite is not there
hours of sleep are few, this whole week has been a blur.
I haven't cared to watch tv or know what day it is
I haven't cleaned or gone to work or took iris to school- I am not me, who is this?
I still have so much to get done
it will get done.
I feel like I'm in a daze, a nightmare at times
I feel like nothing will ever be" normal" again, not this time.

Thankful for my people

I want to thank every single person who has messaged me, texted me, called me,
I want to thank every single person who came to the hospital, stopped by my house, reached out on Facebook and IG
I want to thank every single person who offered help, love and support in all forms,
I have seen them all, I have read them all and I hope you feel heard.
I love them all and I thank you.
Thank you so much, each one of you.
I know that I am loved
I know that my dad is forever loved by all of you and that means just as much.

My memories

life was never perfect right dad? but yet it was
I remember being so young and some of the places you lived and visiting some.
Sometimes I would have bad dreams and you would wake me up and take me to the kitchen for milk and cookies
That is a strong memory that has always stuck with me.
You would hold me on your shoulders and sing "she's my changa-Lena, my changa-leeeena" and id fall asleep on your head
And I would wake up when my chin would hit your head.
I remember loving hanging out with Randy and the family we would take metal detectors and go everywhere looking for "treasure" and that was always a highlight for me.
When my mom didn't take me to get my bellybutton pierced you took me
You held my hand and signed off on the release.
We even wanted to get matching tattoos
but we didn't want to put more ink on our bodies and decided not to.
I remember being little at uncle bennys
You had a camper shell we would ride in-you always told me buckle up even if you are just driving across the street.
That is a lesson I teach my kids because of you

That is something I will forever remember and pass on
thanks to you.
you would always cook chorizo and eggs and I loved it
just recently I made you soy chorizo-it's not how you
made it for me as a child but we enjoyed it.
I remember when you left to Washington and I cried my
eyes out
I thought you would leave and not come back and I didn't
understand like I do now.
you kept telling me you were going to get better
and that you would be back to me, even better than ever.
I thought I'd never see you again but you held true
I had made plans for if you never came back and plans
for the day, I would get to see you.
you cut off your long hair and came back to me
got yourself into salvation army.
With their help you got a job and got back to church
Then you got a car and we became inseparable.
I remember you'd take me to the movies on the bus and
you'd say
(pointing to passing cars)"one day that will be us babe"
and ever since you got a car again
you say pointing at people at the bus stop "remember
when" …
remember when that was us?"

dad I love you. You came so far because of all you gave up. You gave me memories to cherish over my 25 years I'll never forget

I love you so so so so so much, I could never forget.

Angel Saturdays

you were so close to so many
I am on the phone crying with Becky.
she is telling me how you'd always want to hang out
her days off were Saturday and you would tell her
Saturdays are Angel days now
"I have to be with Lena, it's our angel day and I have to be there"
you put us first and last but always first and made that very clear.
because of work the weekends were ours to make the most of
when you stopped working, I started working and we always made time for family fun.
I use to always want you to not work
then it changed to you not wanting me to work.
we always just wanted to do more
that's what life is for.
You would spend your last penny on anyone
you'd say "what? I can't take it with me so I'm spending it" done!

The call from the mortician

I got a call about how to fix your facial hair
they are trying to clean you up-I told them leave you as you are.
The goatee needs to stay, your clothes are there with you
they told me you are at the chapel, I felt like running over there to be next to you.
I am glad you are there, we will all be there in about 5 days
I know it's too far away.
and yet it's still so little time to get so much done
when Michael told me, you were there and Dennis said he was fixing you up…
I felt like I could feel you with me
like you were out for one of your haircuts, you loved to be "clean".
You had been asking for one but been in too much pain to go
Now you are getting one and I am not sure you even know.
dad I love you so much. I wish I could be with you right next to you
Wednesday will be here soon.
I am going to never want to let you go just like on Tuesday I did not want to leave your side in that hospital bed and yet I couldn't stay.

1/24/14

First sign after (day 3 after)

dad ever since I had to leave you in the icu, room 9 at Kaiser hospital
I've been home, I've been to the chapel, I've been sleeping trying to dream of you-trying to find a sign your here around me, trying to see you.
people have said you came to them in their dreams
I've just been waiting for a sign, waiting for you to come back to me....
today while shopping for the kid's outfits for next Wednesday/Thursday
my phone started going off in my pocket, it wouldn't stop vibrating,
I figured a phone call from someone so I went to answer
I picked it up-the screen went black and started flashing on and off-it was so bizarre.
the keyboard came up and the buttons were being pressed on their own
I wanted to take a screenshot or video
But I couldn't, so I quickly went to find Maddie
to show her what was happening.
but she wasn't around and instead of looking for her I just held the phone to watch it
our picture was flashing, the phone took everything off except it.

I knew to myself that you were giving me a sign
you were telling me you were there with me, you have been with me this whole time.
you were showing me my sign I've been waiting for
I smiled and said thank you and the phone went back to normal!
Maddie came back and I told her what happened
And then! Something else happened!
Luther Vandross comes on "never too much"
a song me and you were just listening to singing in the car not long ago.
Maddie said "wow that is weird"
For her to feel that says even more about this being real.
it gave me so much comfort, I needed that
I've been waiting for that.
maybe you were telling me you wanted that song on the cd
or maybe you were confirming that the phone flashing was you, really.
I thank GOD for you continuously
I love you dad, keep visiting me please.
I know so many want you around but please keep coming back to me
Thankful, Grateful, Blessed-healing while hurting.

The day has come

I knew the day would come
we can never be prepared to lose someone we love.
You will live on pain free from here on out
I miss you so much, I know you knew that and I know
you know that, even now.
our last hospital pictures are so sad and hard to see
but they still mean everything to me.
you are a fighter and you fought for years with cancer
and it will never win, never.
you always said either way you win-
when you are here and the day you leave-it's a win situation.
I am thankful that even though this day was sudden
that we all still had time to say goodbye-you gave us all
that option.
you held on until we all got to say what we wanted
you held on for kisses, prayers, company, hugs, hand
holding, stories and the kids.
you held on until you felt complete
and then you went up to heaven with your new wings
and your face showed no more signs of pain
your love forever lives on in us-this pain will be our gain.

1/24/14

Day 4 after

Angel is here, Leo is still up
I feel like my dad has been helping Leo help me, these
past couple of days he seems so grown up.
Especially today with all his kisses, telling me it will be
ok and he loves me
dad was that you in there telling me? using Leo to get to me?
they say our babies see angels easier and faster than us
Tuesday you passed away and we joked how you're never
leaving us.
Leo has your middle name and you laughed and said
yeah and nodded "that's right"
it's been a hard week but I know this is another sign.
tomorrow I plan to get out of the house
do a little less planning and stressing and take all the kids
out.
I need to get to the beach
For some reason it is calling me.
I know you'll be there with us
that's all I want.
We have some hard-beautiful days coming up
the kids deserve to get out, get air and smile before
having to go through what's to come.
there was a point today I got so sad and said

"when will I be a little normal again?"
nothing matters the way it did
nothing is as happy, everything has changed.
but I see a light at the end of this tunnel
trying to stay thankful and find closure little by little.
I'll never stop missing or loving you
but I'm trying to learn to be the me you've always loved me to be, too.

"That's my Lena, that's my Lena, that's my little baby Lena......It's just me and my Lena, me and my Lena.... wherever we go, everyone knows. It's just me and my Lena....my changa-Lena"

I can still hear you singing this to me dad
I love you.
I thank you

1/25/14

Newspaper obituary (day 4 after)

The newspaper is going to be fixed
and ran tomorrow the way it should have been.
that's all I wanted.
Dad you should know, I don't need perfection.
but I do need respect
for you, for me, for our family and all this represents.
I want this as beautiful as your soul
I want you happy and proud as always and I want you to know ...
I am not settling for less than all you deserve and all that we can make happen
I am excited and nervous for this to happen again.

Your brother Everett, my uncle called me
It's been nice getting to know him, getting to know family.
He sounds a lot like you -telling me nothing is perfect, mistakes happen
To worry about the kids, live for the kids, don't stress,
that I am doing the best I can with all of this
and then he ends it with "I'll handle that lady and whatever's wrong Ill fix it"
just like you dad! ...there for me how you would have been.
positive and kind with some protection and father instinct

I will smile today at life and for love support and family.
I will smile tomorrow at today's mistakes being corrected
Blessings in disguise are always present.

Dad if I was rich and if I could, the whole newspaper
would be written about you
There are so many memories to share, so much to share
about you.
I would love to share you with the whole world
but I kept it short and simple.
Not because of price but because all in all you were a
family man loved by so many
and your friends are considered family.
so, in that moment of doing this
I felt it was complete as is.
to make it short and sweet
I have Facebook to write forever about you, to anyone
who wants to hear me speak.
we all have next Wednesday/ Thursday to speak and see you
and we have our whole lives to keep you living on, we
love you.

Fern Kruger and maybe someday you'll write a book

1/25/14

Re-opened wound

Every day is a new struggle, New challenge, New tears, New triumph, New smile, New day
This week it constantly feels like one wound is being repeatedly tore open, in different ways.
It hurts all the same.
ever since this wound was opened it never has had a real chance to heal
and I'm sure it will take forever and I don't even know if healing is really real.
I know people go through these heartaches' way too often
I can't force the healing. I have to just let it happen.
When you closed your eyes for the final time, I lost a piece of my heart and soul
….I lost a piece of my heart and soul.

Our Next-door neighbor came over for Angel iris (their friend)
She said" I heard you grandpa died, but he was so nice, even though We weren't his grandchildren
he still let us call him grandpa and would buy us stuff and take us places too"
that was just you and I am so thankful they got to know you.

We went for a long walk today; it was the hardest ever
Physically and mentally- I couldn't get myself together.
ran into some people we know and got that" I've never
seen you like this, your always smiling and happy"
I'm finding it hard to smile, hard to eat, hard to sleep-
But I'm trying.
Love you dad

Endless infinity

with how hard life has been this week I know next week will be harder
 and at some point, I know it will be easier.
Little by little I am trying to get back to life
ate more today, took a walk, got more stuff for the services done, right now -this is life.
next week iris will go back to school
I requested next week off of work too.
I know I need to slowly ease back into reality
and hopefully find time to take care of me.
I love all of my family and friends
had a talk with my mom today and the tears felt endless.
This is hard on us all
I have some of the best angels in the world up above.

Rest In peace to my loved ones

I am so thankful for all the family I have here on this earth.
I am so thankful my husband and I each still have our mothers.
thank you dad for all you helped me become.
as much as I wish you were here, I am so happy you fought so hard and I am so happy you are not suffering....
MY LOVE FOR YOU IS INFINITY

The kids room, was your room
I am fixing the kids room back up- heartbreaking to say the least
but I am doing this all for them, for me, for you, for life living.
I can't let this million-dollar smile go to waste
See you tomorrow because I don't think I can wait until super bowl Sunday.

1/25/14

Day 5 after
(do you get cremated or buried?)

I wish I knew the right thing to do
I wish I would have had this conversation with you.
I have had two people tell me that you wanted to be cremated
to save me some money, that you had life insurance so that I could have money left over for me and the kids.
Although we had hard talks about knowing when it was time to let go
you never told me if you wanted to be buried or cremated-it's unknown.
In my heart, my first instinct told me you want to be buried where your mom is and family.
We would visit them there and you always talked about wanting to visit them more
With you there I know that people can visit you, I feel like that matters more.
If you were cremated, I know that I could keep you right here
still in the house forever with me but would that be fair?
Thoughts have me a bit torn
money is not my issue, respecting your wishes are.

The spot we picked for you is in the middle of two statues
You are facing the hills where the cows roam and the birds fly high-it reminds us of you.
I think you would love it; I just wish I knew
I just wish I knew the right thing to do.
I never want to feel as though you wouldn't be proud or happy
Maybe I would find more comfort in keeping you right here in the house, with me.
I miss you and wish we would have had these hard talks now
I know its never ideal but I don't know what to do now.

one thing I feel content about is my dad's trust in me
trust in my choices/heart and instincts.
watching the news, so many people leave us every second of the day
and some in the worst ways.
A lot of us never get to say goodbye
I find so much thankfulness that we had that chance with our time.
your last words stuck in my head "I love you...I love you more..."
It's in my head forever, tell me I get to always remember.

"hi Catrina....hi Steve...Iris!...Leo...Angel!..amen"
you said what you wanted...most of it.

Sorry we couldn't understand some of it
you asking for a spit cup because you often had congestion.
wanting to use the bathroom but you couldn't leave your hospital bed
you deserved to leave that bed.
our last moments were the hardest and yet the best
because it broke me to see you struggle and suffer and it brings me peace to know you get to rest.
we were all with you, you got your wish of that
you went from not being able to talk to being able to say you love me one last time-you gave me that.
You got to see us and hear us as you transitioned into heaven
I will forever have a piece of me missing and I will forever have gratitude for that transition.
I know you will be watching over us and I just am so happy for life
I will continue making you proud and taking care of us the way you would-only the best, right?
I love you and I am going to live life to the fullest
like we always did but more like you did.
you set the standards oh so high dad
thank you. Always giving me someone to look up to,
now I look up to the sky.

1/26/14

Thankful memories

Dad. I love all of our memories

I am glad I am a picture fanatic because right now it's really helping me.

I love the videos, hearing your voice

Why didn't I take more?

you took me to buy my wedding dress, get my belly button pierced

you drove us to Disneyland, got me a job at Connolly's as a greeter.

your first place you got big enough so I could have a room that was about 9 years ago

you always said we should live together, what if something happened to you one day

I have a feeling you always had a feeling that one day we would see this day.

I have this thought that you knew way sooner about your condition than you let me believe

I always felt so close like I knew something.

all loved ones knew you were given two years but you made it to three

what kept you going through all that pain and suffering?

me and you are two of the same
I think we've always been on the same page.
we lived life normal, happy, with faith
we had hope and love that this would all work out in its own way.
That's how we lived forever
No one could take away the positive way we chose to live. Not doctors or cancer.
sure, it's hard, there's pain and tears
but we smiled and treated everyday like it was the last day here.
Never crippled by any setbacks
I am you; you are me so I know you'll forever be right here where I am.

Costs of dying

I know you told people you don't want me spending money
I would clear out my whole bank account for you, honestly.
I know you know this; I know you knew this
It's also not realistic with costs we know nothing about such as this.
we often went shopping and id buy you whatever you wanted with a smile on my face
you were the same.
Making "in memory cards". Making t-shirts. Making banners. making Posters.
Buying cake. Making slideshows. Putting together digital frames and getting music together.
Figuring out food. Who's buying what, who's making what
How to honor you.
Getting outfits together, with the help of others I will get through this
with you as my angel I will get through this.
I am just like you when it comes to money
we can't take it with us, you spend what you have to on what you need.
Then you buy what you want if you can afford to do so
I want this to be as beautiful as it can be, it will be so,

I know it will all work out
thank you to all who have asked to help out.
I need and will accept all the help I can get
(which usually isn't like me, or my dad! Haha, had to get that laugh in.)
but I know all the love and support we have
I want anyone to help, I want anyone to get the healing that they can.
I want the word spread so anyone and everyone can make it Wednesday/Thursday.
I want the very best for you dad, today and always.
I will spend as much as my wallet allows
It will all work out, someway-somehow.

1/26/14

Making News, Again (Day 5 After)

Although it came out yesterday
My dad's obituary is out today.
the unrevised copy was sent out on accident
I thank my angels and GOD because that means we now have two days of sharing him.
This means more people are reading about my dad
So yes, you continue to touch lives one way or another-even while in heaven.
This world was a better place with you, my life is not the same without you here,
my love stays strong, always and forever.
My dad's family in Washington and Modesto don't get the paper
So, I ask loved ones for support.
If you can buy a few copies please do so
I too am going to purchase some, I never ever do so.
(East Bay 2 package which consist of Oakland Tribune, Alameda Times Star, Daily Review, Argus and Tri-Valley Herald.)

there's a lot of my dad's family I don't know
It is so hard to write an obituary when you don't know.
while the obituary was being done, I felt so lost

I met a couple of his sisters and Washington family a couple of times but not enough.
Not as much as I would have wished for by now
I want so badly to make everyone feel loved and proud.
I have been able to have shared some phone calls or even cards but not enough
sorry if I don't know many of you by face or name, this is really tough.
sorry that a loss has to bring us together
I hope to get to know a lot of you even if only through social media and painful get togethers.
I hope you share memories and pictures with me
I hope we can all become closer and create new memories.
I hope to get to know my cousins, my dad's nieces and nephews
I hope to get to know my aunts and uncles too.
I wish my dad was here to be a part of what the years will hold for us
I know he's up above so proud and happy to see all of this love.
His love is still working its magic in so many ways
I love you dad. Forever and always.
In my heart and all that I do
You are me and I am you.

1/26/14

Can't walk it off

I have been trying to walk places, well not trying- I have
I know for some that may be hard to understand.
Not everyone feels grief the same
Its all new for me too, every step of the way.
I have walked places yesterday and today
it's been so hard but it was needed today.
as more and more gets done on this long list of things "I want to do",
I am finding it easier to walk, before I wasn't able to.
there were days I could barely move
couldn't eat, couldn't drink, couldn't smile-that was the mood.
huge lack of taking pictures, not cooking
couldn't do my normal things I do. It is literally like I lost a huge part of my heart and soul and identity.
these things are still difficult for me
but it's been almost a week.
I am slowly getting better at things that use to be natural for me
I am slowly coming back to me.
I want Wednesday and Thursday to be beautiful, I am trying my best to get done all that comes to mind
I have been blessed to have 2 weeks off with pay (sick/vacation/bereavement) days, I have been blessed with time.

I have been blessed with family and friends stopping by helping me with the stress load and helping me find my way slowly through this new journey of mine.
This new journey that is not just mine
This new part of life, that is the end of one's life.
I still have a few things to get done
I am thankful for how far we have already come
These last 6 days have been too much
And yet, it's never enough.
thank you, dad, for always being here for me
even when you left to claim your wings.
you remain here for me and helping me
you have brought so many wonderful people into my life; I will soon meet family I haven't had the chance to really meet.
You continue to work your magic still and I love you for everything
I know I have a long way to go until I'm ok but I'm on my way, I am forward moving.
you have given me so much-taught me so much and I know I can only become better:
more forgiving, more loving, more everything I already am, but better.
When I say better, I mean a higher version of myself
I am never going to lose who I am because I know you're a big piece of that, and I will always have your help.

Clothes in a box

My husband and I are going through all your clothes
so many we are going to keep, and some, we won't.
some I am going to save in a bag in a box
to try to save your smell-I don't want to lose that piece I
have of you left. I have already lost so much.
I found a shirt with my 8th grade graduation picture on it
it said proud dad-made me almost break down but I tried
to contain it.
The raider jersey I got you with your number 7 and your
name on the back
oh, how I miss you and wish you could come back.
So many clothes that eventually family will get to take
This just all feels so wrong but I know it was a decision I
had to make.
Every step of this is so hard
I love you; I miss you-with all of my heart.

1/26/14

Last Monday day 6 after

its Monday,1 week since you were rushed to alameda hospital
Iris is finally back in school.
Edgardo is wearing your chain and sweater
Leo and I are here.
I feel like time is flying already and yet still going so slow
I miss you and I love you-seems to be all I really know.
I wish this part of life wasn't a part of life
but it is and I know you are my angel and I know we have to make the most of life.
It's hard without you but there's still so much I thank GOD for
For our before, my now and so much hope for the future.
life is too short-I've always known that
I love you, always and forever, dad.

A pain that money, shopping, showers and sleep can't fix
A pain that words, love and support can't change. It is what it is.
A pain like no other. A total shutdown
you don't just lose the one who left but you lose yourself and, in some ways, those around.

Healing While Hurting

You have to find a way to pick up the pieces and rebuild
and keep going
You have to learn to live again, healing while hurting.

there's no medicine or cure for this
no band aid for it.
just have to hope time heals all even if it never heals
just hope with time it gets easier- even if that isn't really real.

Not so fortunate

I know that I have been blessed to have you in my life this long,
I know some people aren't so fortunate
I know I'm blessed you've made it this far,
some people aren't so fortunate.
I know your faith, love and spirit are strong, some people don't have what you do
I know Your tired dad, but I am not ready to lose you.
I still need to take you for that pedicure
and I know you wanted to see monster jam and motorcycles
and you have been putting off our family pictures.
We still have so much living to do, I'm not leaving your side,
cancer does not get to have you. I love you. I'm here.

Who you were, who you are

The deacon called today,
I told him about the man you are
I have to tell him about you
So, when he speaks, you will be honored.
I am getting pictures together for a slideshow to show
I am looking for cloth tablecloths so that it will be set up nicely at the reception
I ordered a banner at Walgreens and its ready for pick up
I made several different cards with pictures and prayers- also ready for pick up
Everyday there's a list of things to get done
I miss you so much.
Every phone call breaks my heart
every step of this is so hard.
I thank everyone for everything
there's no way I could do it all on my own. Alone isn't what you would want for me.

DD214

one of the biggest pieces of information we are waiting
for is the dd214 for my dad to come in
to show proof of honorable discharge when he was in the marines.
does any family know how to help with this?
I know nothing about any of this.
But I do know it exists
Thanks to my grandpas' service.
the chapel has sent an emergency fax
but so far hasn't received anything back.
if the dd214 comes in then the marines will do a special piece at the cemetery
if it does not come in then the California honor guard will do something.
with the dd214 there will be a special headstone and
some special moments for me and my dad at the service
doesn't that sound special, doesn't that sound worth it?

1/27/14

Day 7 after

Iris asks,
She's only 7-how do I have the answers for these questions.

" mom when I die will I see grandpa? "
"Does he have a bed in heaven? "
"Where is he sleeping?"
"How do you sleep in the sky? "
Will he see me sing tomorrow? "
"I was scared to hug him because I don't want him to hurt."
"what will he wear"
"When we see him again?"
"Will he stay asleep?"

I still have my moments, when I want to walk by to check on you
I still have my moments- when I want to call out "what?" because I hear you.
I want to call you to see if you need anything
I hope your warm enough, you were always cold most recently.
I hope you're not hungry, lately a bite or 2 would do the trick

you kept saying how it's going to be a good year; this year has only just started.
I only had you here for 21 days this year
I'm thankful and yet I wish we had even more time
I just can't believe this is real.

One week ago

Today I have so much to do and yet I'm finding it so
hard to get out of bed
Me and Leo are still laying here, sleeping as much as
possible-I can't get out of my own head.
One week ago today was the worst day, when we were
asked (me and you) What you wanted to do
Continue on machines or to be comfortable with family
to say our goodbyes and you chose option number two.
You chose to be comfortable
they say you left us at 12:40 last Tuesday.
we stayed hours later
your body was still warm but getting colder.
Your eyes wouldn't open, your chest stopped moving
the breath in your oxygen mask was no longer showing.
I had to leave your side, I had to sign papers
I had to let your hand go and I was just trying to
remember all there was to remember.
Like the warmth of your hair and the feel of your hair
The sound of your voice and the people that were there.

It's been one week today and it doesn't get easier
it's been a constant wound that continues to be reopened
and hopefully after Thursday will have some time to heal
better.

I love you dad.
I wish I could bring you back.
I know your happy, proud and pain free
I know you did not want to leave.
I know you felt it was time because if you didn't, you'd still be here fighting
You fought long with a smile and left it all to GODS timing.
I will try to fight and heal with a smile but I know it will be awhile until I can
You would sometimes say "are you a Mexican or a mexiCANT?"

The you, you left behind

The past few days, little by little I have been going
through the you that you left behind
in forms of clothes, letters, cards, pictures, videos, cell
phones, wallets, fb, awards, material items that I could
find.
it's so very hard to keep some stuff and throw some away
I want to respect your privacy and learn more about you
in new ways.
Going through this whole process is hard, for so many
reasons why

My Angel here on earth, my dad, my hero, my mirror,
my heavenly guardian angel
I love you.
I know life wasn't easy for you, you went through a lot,
I saw some of your downfalls,
I heard stories of your hard times,
I watched you change your life
and although you ended up having cancer-
it was all uphill for us.
we enjoyed life.
You enjoyed life
and taught me so much just by being you.

Emergency form

I sit here in happy tears
Appreciating all the good that is right here.
last week the chapel put in an emergency form for your dd214
I know not everyone may know what that means.
I had to do my own research and learning
I had to investigate and ask questions for understanding.
yesterday nothing had come in and so they sent out another emergency form
-this time with your obituary and picture.
I have been searching through all of your belongings to find this "little blue paper"
It was something I was told to look for.
I have come across your book "marine corps recruit depot, San Diego California third battalion, platoon 3107"
I came across a little blue paper with the same info, and I just know you are with me while in heaven.
there are pictures of you in this book, I call the chapel to see if your dd214 has come in,
they say there is a note that says "ok with honors", am I finally able smile again?
I am so happy and proud that you will get all you deserve even as you be laid to rest, you still are seen for your work and honor.

I was told with a dd214 you will receive (I will on your behalf) a flag
and that the marines will do a tribute to you at the cemetery (I am more than ok with that.)
They say this means that you will have a special headstone
I was told without it you would receive a California honor guard tribute.

BUT I WAS TOLD ITS IN DAD! ITS IN!
I AM SO PROUD OF YOU AND WITH THIS…..
I ASK PLEASE, FAMILY AND FRIENDS FEEL FREE TO TAKE PICTURES AND VIDEOS TOMORROW AND THURSDAY.I WOULD LOVE THEM, more than you can know.

Somebody help me

when does the stress end, when can my heart and Brain relax?
Just got a call that the insurance hasn't gone through, I thought we were done worrying about finance.
they need more papers, I have to sign stuff
last Tuesday I was told not to worry; it's taken care of.
I know it will all work out but these headaches are crazy
I've had so many changes and mix ups, it's becoming too much lately.
It just hurts.
But nothing will ruin anything.
Everything will work.
Its all going how it is meant to be.
I have faith, I have you and positivity
Love you dad, thank you for always looking out for me.

1/28/14

Your eyes

posting the photos and videos from my dad's cell phone to his Facebook
I have his information to do so but I promise I won't snoop.
hope this helps loved ones and myself see through his eyes
I hope it helps to see how happy he was and is with GOD, with life.
I am leaving his profile and cover as he had it
I want his fb to still be his in every way, I just wanted to share service information.
I want to reach his friends list that isn't mine
I want to reach all loved ones, hopefully in time.
I promise to respecting the privacy
And after this, you won't see any more posts from him through me.

1/28/14

Day 8 after: VIGIL

Some little girls grow up not knowing or meeting their fathers
I know I have to be thankful
some lose their dad's before they understand what it means
I know I have to be grateful.
some people don't get a chance to say goodbye when heaven calls,
some people couldn't fight as long.
on this day I am trying so very hard to be thankful dad.
I am thankful for the 25 years you and I had.
I am thankful you got to walk me down the aisle,
You got to meet 3 of your grandchildren and make it worthwhile.
for over 6 years you were able to be in their lives
I wish it was more but I will be thankful for the time.
you fought cancer for 3 years
even when they said not to expect more than 2 years.
you gave us the chance to all say goodbye
you did that, you held on and you didn't leave until we all got that time.
You didn't leave us until you had that time with us
You fought till the very end, you did it so calm.
You were only 52 looking 40,

of course, I feel heaven took you from us all too soon-you had more years to do living.
But that wasn't our reality
And it wasn't meant to be our story.
I am trying to be strong and thankful
And I am praying today is as beautiful as your soul.

We will see you tomorrow, no matter how hard it will be, there's no place I'd rather be.

Vigil-ualize

I am strong, I am hopeful and I am happy but dad, I am already breaking down
I am not sure I am strong enough to be happy or strong today, I feel it all now.
I went inside and came right back out
instant tears when trying to get t-shirts out.
Turning the music on, trying to get the slideshow going
Getting the reception room set up
Smiling while crying.
to have slideshows, music, open casket in one place
no dad I am not strong enough, I have no poker face.
I don't care to have it all together
I can't care with these feelings taking over.
I love you and miss you so much, but as hard as it will be there's no place I'd rather be
than by your side
celebrating your life
and celebrating the wonderful man and Angel You are….
Easier said than done, that means any of this has an "easier"

I couldn't stop touching your hair
because I feel like that was the only thing that still felt real.

Your hair is the last real part that still feels like you
I'm so sorry your so ice cold, I brought a blanket for you.
you looked good naturally
you did not look like the you last Tuesday in the hospital
and today is an even different you I see.
Almost 5 hours. Your body is so hard,
Your skin is so cold and makeup is covering your scars
The scars that make you-YOU
I feel like the scene in "my girl" where she's screaming,
he needs his glasses, I want to tell them to wipe off the
makeup because I want to see YOU

The chapel people didn't tell us only certain computers
work for the slideshow
so, we didn't have one, even though we had one-I am
upset but I can let go.
the ribbon on the flowers were blank
you looked handsome as always.
the programs, the shirts and the cards went fast
I am sad and thankful for that.
thank you to all who spoke, thank you to all who came
thank you for all the love and support-for wearing his
smile and sharing the pain.
see you again in the morning.

my eyes won't stop burning,
I still feel like this isn't real
Please tell me, in time I will heal.

Oh, how I miss you
see you in the morning dad. I love you.

1/29/14

Day 9 after: funeral

1 hour to go, this is happening too fast.
A bad dream that I can't wake up from and yet I want this time to last.
going through the motions and moments but it doesn't feel real
I know today will hurt the worst and I know today I will also heal.
Leaving at 9 to make sure your music and slideshow works today
See you all at 11, I look forward to being together in this way.
Last Tuesday was it.
I held your hand and tried to soak in the feeling of it.
I felt your heart beat
I saw you breathe.
Last Tuesday your skin was warm
 you looked like you-only tired.
today you look so different- its all a new scene
Today feels unreal, it's all a completely different sight and feelings.

I may be the picture queen but not today, not today at all
Laid to rest, it was beautiful.

You are handsome.

Your right next to the hills, the cows, 2 statues, children playing soccer right below.

Flowers lay where you rest

I don't want to leave you again.

Thank you to every single person who came, it was beautiful to see so many cars behind us, loved ones besides us.

YOU DID THIS DAD,

like you always do

Cemetery

we got to the cemetery,
your music was playing
you had a special tribute-even though I thought it be bigger
I appreciated what it was, I appreciate the honor.
I didn't get to release my dove
I wanted everyone to feel loved and thought of.
I enjoyed watching loved ones do it for me
I have your flag and I just know you're up there smiling.
proud of yourself-I'm so proud of you.
I feel you deserved so much more
but I feel so blessed to have all those cars following behind for you.
I feel so thankful to all who took off work or came sick today
to everyone who came from near and far, everyone who found a way.
some of you drove from Washington, Sacramento, Tracy, Modesto-
my dad is so loved and he loved you all.
I had so many say "look at all he brought together"
and others come despite of feelings towards one another.
thank you to all who brought, bought and made food

thank you for those who gave cards-even money too.
Thank you to anyone who bought a shirt made of him
Thank you to all who wore a shirt in honor and
representation.
Thank you all who gave time today
It will forever mean everything to me, it really helps with
pain.
thank you all so much to the pallbearers, to everyone
I know my dad has to be smiling at all the love from
everyone.

1/30/14

Dads at the funeral

seeing my family members with their dads,
taking pictures, hugging, smiling together-some even laugh.
it hurts me as I sit here
sitting here in my tears.
It's not jealousy-or maybe it is
I do not feel anything except hurt and hopeful
intentions.
I just hope that all my friends and loved ones who have
their dads
can make the best of everyday like my dad and I did.
I wish everyone could have the relationship my dad and
I did
I know everyone's situations are different.

we took our last picture today
and it's the hardest moment ever watching you lay.
kissing your cold forehead, feeling your hand not hold
mine back
not being able to look in your eyes or hear you talk to me
back.
all that was normal was touching your hair
All that was normal is that nothing is normal- this new
normal doesn't feel fair.

I love you dad. I miss you.
I will be visiting you this weekend; I know you will too.
Superbowl Sunday-where else would I be
The only place that feels right, is now the cemetery.

9 days ago

last tuesday,9 days ago-you left your physical body
that day, I lost a piece of me.
the very next morning I was at the chapel of roses
making funeral arrangements
I was at the cemetery picking out your resting spot and it had to be perfect.
every day since then I have been busy getting a vigil and funeral put together
(I didn't know anything about anything when it came to this), now I know more than before.
I'd still make it all better if I could.... some ask how I did it
some commend me on all I did.
in reality, it's been hard
I wouldn't live with myself if I didn't try my best for you, with all my heart.
I only had you in mind the whole time
it all feels like a movie or something, so unreal-all the time.
even though there's moments it hits me hard smack in the face
it feels like "why is this happening to me, to you-why is this your fate?"
I know I am blessed; I am thankful and I am still standing
I know to be grateful, to live life to the fullest-not just for you but for me.

a parent like you with reasons to live, reasons to fight, reasons to smile, reasons to be proud
I cannot stay feeling down.
I am always in a "fix it" mode and this is something I can't fix
but yet I'm still trying to do all that I can to fix it as best as I can-I cant shake those intentions.
I don't know how this all works-I know it does
but I just can't believe you are gone.
I know, you are still right here
But right here is different that when you were physically here.
it's going to take my whole life to try to get use to this
who says I have to get use to this?
Can I heal without "getting use to this"?
Can I move on with acceptance while still dealing with it?
you will forever live on with me
I'm never letting you go. Not ever. I'm holding on to your energy.
I love you and can't wait to see you this weekend
That line now means something so different.
But I feel it and mean it just the same
We all want to be with you and can't wait.
I can't wait to see you
in family, in the kids, in the sky, in my dreams and in all that I do.

I promise to keep it all together down here as best as I can
Like I always have.

rest in peace my guardian angel.
I'm glad you've always known how much you mean to me.
I'm glad we have no regrets.

Father Jim Frank

what I really got from father Jim frank today: we are not throw aways,
we all will die some day
but we live on-we can't just be thrown away

I have not yet been baptized but it was always in the plan
I promise it will happen soon dad.
It's something I've always wanted to do
I need to start figuring out how and do it, make it true.
If I can get through these past 2 weeks-
I can find my way with that, definitely.
I love you dad
Always and forever
Forever and always

1/30/14

Day 10 after

the doctor who has been your liver doctor the past few
years just called me
he heard you had passed away; He wanted to call me and
tell me how he was sorry.
He said that he hopes you weren't suffering
(of course, I am instantly crying.)
he said you always talked about me and the kids at every
visit
that he knows we meant everything to you. (he didn't
have to share these comments, I am so thankful he did,)
He says he knows how important prayers and GOD is to
you
he says you will be missed by all of the doctors and
nurses-they all felt connected to you.
 you were such a great man and that you fought longer
and harder than most
even he didn't expect you to go.
he was expecting to see you for your next operation
which would have been today
dad, you touched every person you met and you
continue to touch lives even as you are away.

Round table

We spent New Year's Eve here
you were tired and in pain but refused to rest or stay home.
if you were able, you did it!
Didn't want you to miss out on anything.
last Monday I was here and that's when you started
slipping away from us.
anytime we went out
I'd bring you something back, knowing you couldn't eat
it all but it's the thought and action that counts.
I love you dad. We miss you.
memories live on
the last picture of us all together, while you were
physically still with us, was here.
Round table.

Already an Angel

you were here and you were already an angel.
you already had wings, they just couldn't be seen
you will always be my hero and role model of what
strength and love means.
you were always the best dad no matter your occupation
or way of life
I always thought highly of you, I was always proud of
you, no such thing as wrong or right.
you always looked out for everyone
you changed your whole life for me, for us.
you changed your life and GOD let you stick around for
the blessings
for graduations, grandchildren, and my wedding.
GOD kept you here,
although fighting cancer was a struggle
he gave you strength to smile
GOD gave you strength to see life in another way
What a beautiful reason to live fully every day.
we made the most of life before we knew you were sick,
we have always made the most of life every time we were
together.
dad I love you, I can't say it enough
my guardian angel-I'll always wish you were here and it
will never be enough.

I am so thankful for the memories
and I am so happy you are not in any more pain.
dad I love you.
thank you for loving me.
I have to think of it as your just not here, not next to me for the moment
that you are somewhere and you are happy -smiling the way you always did.
I know you are still protecting me
I don't have to see you physically to know you are taking care of me.
I know I can't call you, can't cook for you, can't help brush your hair,
I know I can't help put on your socks, I can't hug you or talk to you- like when you were here.
I can do all of those things, just
...not in the same ways I did before....
I have to believe that yes you are gone but you are still here.

1/31/14

1 Month Since You've Been Gone

today makes one month since you've been gone.
One month without your texts and calls.
One month without conversations, hugs, anything
One month without taking pills, asking for help, one
month without you suffering.
One month without all I had gotten used to
Still doesn't feel real most of the time, Sometimes I still
believe I will see you.
I really need to make a new shirt because I've worn this
one all month
It's the only one I have right now-that I really love.
that last hospital visit is all too fresh in my memory
woke up from a dream with you, but it was just a dream.
It was very short but I know you were here with me for
that moment
in my dream we were walking and I was looking at you
saying I love you so much dad and you said I know it.
"I love you too babe but I have to go"
then you called Edgardo to take my hand
you kept walking as we couldn't catch up
and then the kids needed us

and the dream changed into something else.
I love you so much. I miss you so much.
I'm trying not to cry but it's so hard with how much you mean to me and all of us.

2/21/14

2 months without you

today makes 2 months without you
how is time flying so fast without you?
January 21, 2014 was the strongest I've ever been
was the most selfless I've ever been, was the saddest I've ever been.
doctors gave me two options:
to keep you on machines or to give you comfort as you pass on to heaven.
I brought you those two choices because you were able to hear, understand and respond
I wanted you to choose because I know you'd choose what you felt was right for you (only you knew more than anyone.)
you chose to be comfortable; you chose to be taken off of machines,
to be surrounded with love-to let go-ultimately.
At 25 years old as your only child I was not ready for that
but I started calling people because I had to meet that request.
no matter how hard situations were for me-I know they were harder for you
you were the one who was suffering, you were the one who had to accept this too.

instead of keeping you to myself for those last hours and moments
I shared you with over 20 people, in one room- it was the best decision.
I shared space with people who helped me be strong
Loved ones who helped comfort you, who love you and loved us.
when the funeral came around, I made collages of you
even with my love of pictures and my love for you
I gave those collages away to your sisters
because although it's hard for me, as your daughter
I know it's hard for them as well
I wanted everyone to feel loved and special.
I had emptied my bank account to make t-shirts for everyone
because I wanted everyone to have that piece of you, to spread your face around,
for you to live on.
The t-shirts were meant to show love and support
I always tried to make you proud, even when it hurts.
I've always wanted you happy
You are not here but I know you are at peace.
2months ago I know exactly where my strength and selflessness came from-it came from you
you are a piece of my heart and soul that can never be replaced or erased, I am you.

I love you so much dad and days aren't easy
I know your body is buried but you aren't gone to me.
I miss everything about you but I know you'd never leave me
You will always be around, yes, spiritually.
all of this is so hard to accept and deal with
know I'm never letting you go, even when it's hard to deal with.
I have my shirt on, like I do many days,
my bracelet on and your smile on my face.
Two months ago, was the strongest we both have ever been
The most understanding and the most selfless.
you live on in me
you live on because of many.

3/21/14

Cancer

You weren't supposed to leave so soon
Some might say you weren't" suppose" to make it so long
Cancer has no sympathy
Cancer has no cure for some
You were an angel here already, the day you left you got your wings
Here or there, you'd always say either way you are winning
You are my dad forever, forever and always
I will love you forever, in my heart you'll forever stay
Pictures in frames, pictures on shirts, pictures on bracelets and in my memory
No picture can replace the living you but they do help comfort me
I wish we had more time but time is not guaranteed for any of us
I wish angels could be seen every time we looked up
I will take you with me everywhere I go because I am so much like you
You live on in me and in all the people who knew you too
I love you dad, always and forever
Daddy's little girl, forever and ever

3/7/14

3 months Without You

today makes 3 months since you've been gone and every day is so hard
Today is easter Monday, it does feel extra hard.
not a day has passed where I haven't cried
not one single day in three months has been one of dry eyes.
Not a single day has been without pain being present
where I haven't smiled and felt pain from it.
that last weekend, those last days you were here-is often relived in my mind
I can't stop replaying those painful moments as if it was happening in real time.
as much as I wish you were here, I am happy you are at peace
because watching you those last days was so hard for me.
to see you in so much pain not being able to use the restroom or eat
to watch you unable to feel comfort was the most horrific thing I've ever seen.
seeing you cry and hearing you not be able to say the things you wanted to say
it all broke my heart, in so many different ways.
you left and a huge part of my heart went missing
it was as if I lost you and I lost me,

you left and my smile got smaller
my life changed forever.
The kids ask for you and ask questions
sometimes I can't answer because I just don't have the
answer, but sometimes I just can't get past my own sadness.
we all miss you so much
sometimes I feel like you're not really gone.
Sometimes I really feel your absence
and sometimes I'm angry, sometimes I'm broken.
sometimes I'm strong, sometimes I'm accepting
sometimes I just can't accept the truth, sometimes I can't
stop the tears from falling.
I remember that day that started the last days
running to the sounds of the ambulance to get to you
before they could take you away.
screaming please don't leave me, yes, I was screaming at
the sky
I probably looked crazy to all the cars and people passing by.
sometimes I still want to scream at the top of my lungs
for heaven not to take you
then other moments I'm just so thankful, that I was ever
able to have time with you.
thankful you didn't leave me sooner or in any other
circumstance
you gave me the gift of time, until the very end.
you fought long and didn't let cancer take you on its time

you held on waiting for everyone to be by your side.
You held on for everyone to find a little peace in goodbye
While you were going through this transition you
continued to give, as if everything were fine.
Here I am 3 months later still trying to get your burial
spot at peace
the headstone is still a process that's incomplete.
There's still so much id give to have 1 more hug
one more talk, watch a movie, or even put your socks on.
I wish I could cook for you once more
go for a ride once more, anything-once more.
have another moment
but 3 months in its still hard to accept, that is a wish that
won't have such fulfillment.

4/21/14

4 months without you

today makes 4 months since I saw you take your last breath
since I saw your eyes close for the last time
since I had to see your spirit leave your body.

nothing hurts more than not hearing your voice
not getting your hug
not having you here.
nothing hurts more than when I had to sit helpless by that hospital bed
knowing I was losing you and that there was nothing I could do
I am so good at thinking fast, fixing things and planning things
I couldn't save you or fix that day or prepare for all these days ahead without you.
not one day has passed that I haven't cried,
that I haven't asked why,
that I don't get mad and sad and wish for you back.
life will never be the same without you.
it breaks my heart when the kids ask when can we visit you
they ask when will the doctors make you better and why did you have to die.
I love you so much dad and miss you more than words can say.

wearing my shirt today like I do many days
with my bracelet on and digital frame playing
and I wish I could wear your million-dollar smile on my face
in time I know I will
but as for now my sadness is here
and I just wish I never had to watch you leave
but I am thankful we all got to make your last wish come true
I am thankful you weren't alone while moving on to heaven.
you will forever live on in me
and a part of me will forever have left with you.

5/21/14

5 months without you

sometimes I catch myself still trying to do things to make you happy and feel better
sometimes I forget you're not here

6/18/14

earlier I walked in the house and burst into tears,
 kind of expecting you to be here and it broke my heart that you are not physically here.

6/7/14

You are the bridge-
To family I see because of you
To the family that I never knew
Trips we didn't take
Connections I didn't make
You are the reason
For my grandpa and family
With you gone, how will I cross that bridge without you next to me
You remain the bridge of connection
But now I have to do more, now family has to choose to be in connection

10/9/20

6 months

There's the piece of me that hates to see you in pain
And the bigger part of me that never wants to see you go or lose you
But my heart tells me it's up to you, even if that means we must say goodbye
When cancer is involved its ok to get too tired to fight
Just let me know if you need me to fight for you
Because I will fight hard if you need or want me to
But I will also let you be at peace and rest if you need or want or ask me to stop fighting
Cancer never wins, never
It made us stronger, live to the fullest, see life in a new light
We all will go one day for different reasons
It seems like everyone gets cancer
I hope the day comes when it never exists anymore
I love you always and forever
Cancer can never take that away
Today makes 6months since you've been gone and it doesn't get any easier

7/21/14

7 months without you

tears fall from my eyes as I read a post someone wrote
As I laugh at the memory that was shared
I'm still not able to laugh without crying
As good as the good times were
It hurts that much more
As much as I need that laugh
I just really need and want you back
As I sit here sick, not feeling good
I can hear your voice in my head
I can see you rushing to my side
...tears fall from my eyes....
You're not here to tell me it will be ok
To tell me you're ok
To tell me you love me
All I want is you to hug me

8/14/14

8 months without you

You always told me if I love it you love it,
if I'm sad from it your sad,
if I'm mad your mad,
if I feel it you feel it.
You were ok with all of my decisions and choices
you always said you knew I deserve the best
and if I'm happy so are you
...I miss u so much....
I haven't been myself since u left 8 months ago...

Thank u dad...for so many amazing people you put in
my life and heart....
8months today and it still hurts like January 21st
what do you say when your kids say daily I miss grandpa
We went here with grandpa
Grandpa use to do this with us and for us
...today they were going through your bin and found
your tattoos and put them on....
8months tomorrow and I still cry like a baby at least once
a day
because I just miss my dad.... we love u

9/21/14

Meant to be

Hearing you say you love me
Seeing people enter the room, hearing you greeting
I thought to myself this can't be it
This can't be the end, can it?
Looking in your eyes, I knew I was losing you
Tears slowly coming from your eyes, you knew too
How do you get comfortable knowing you're going away
How can you be comfortable in so much pain
Moments of watching you make recovery steps gave me so much hope
Moments watching you suffer, hurt me the most
Sleepless nights seeing you unable to eat, unable to speak clear
I was trying to be strong for you, I was trying to hide my fear
But I never felt right to lie, to say I knew we'd be ok
I hoped we would , I prayed for it, I put my trust in faith
I told myself whatever happens that it was meant to be
There's a reason for everything, even if it's hard to see
.....I love you dad
Reliving those last moments haunts me at night
Brings tears to my eyes.
there's no comfort for that.... I just wanted to save you,
I'll never know why cancer had to take you

9/2/14

9 months

9months today since the angels took you away
You decided you could no longer stay
I know it hurt you to leave by the tears in your eyes
I know it hurt you to stay by the pain in your cries
I'm so sorry I couldn't save you,
I wish i was a match
I'm so sorry love couldn't save you
You'd be here if it was that easy
Your smile lives on not only through pictures
But through me and the kids forever
You'll never be forgotten
You'll forever be missed and loved
I wish you were here, you'd be so proud and protective
I wish cancer never existed

10/21/14

Old enough to not know better

old enough to know death is a part of the circle of life
smart enough to know we can't stay forever
but that doesn't make losing you any easier
it doesn't make the pain any better
I see elderly people and can't help but think that should be you-you should be here that long and I should be taking care of you
cancer takes so many lives, all ages, all stages-it is not prejudice
still young enough to want my dad
strong enough to accept reality
weak enough to wish for different
real enough to understand it all
 I miss you so much dad....I know you don't want me to cry but for the past 9 months it seems to happen every day no matter how hard I try not to
I love you
thank you for being strong and brave enough to fight as long as you did, as hard as you did
you would tell me with every operation that you were scared to be put to sleep , scared to not wake up
you would tell me no one knows what it's like to be in your shoes and go through all you had to

you would tell me so much and i just appreciate your honesty, your lack of honesty, your smile, your wisdom, your faith and your love.

10/7/14

26 and still wishing

26 years old
I guess I'm not too old to get my hopes up
Or to wish all these calls would be from you
Old enough to know better
But young enough to still dream the impossible
forever a daddy's girl
today is the first day since the funeral 9months ago that I put on those CDs. I cried all morning because I just can't help it and if I feel it I do it. I miss you dad. All the time, every day. This birthday could never be perfect without you here. I love you. I know you want me happy and I am but I will forever be incomplete. That's just reality. See you again one day but I'm sure you're watching over me to make sure it's no time soon. Love u, always and forever

10/15/14

Tamales

a year of firsts....today was iris and angels first birthday party without you in 7 years
today one child mentioned "so there won't be tamales"
some visitors came and felt like they'd see you here still
some visitors came and it wasn't the same seeing them without you here
MY BLANKET-A PICTURE OF YOU-HUNG IN THE MIDDLE OF THE TOP OF OUR PARTY AND YOU WERE THERE WITH US ALL. Front row center to the pinata showdown where all the kids had a blast. Smiles lit up the back yard.
I would look up and see you there and at times I could feel your hand on my shoulder.
thank you for being with us dad, today and forever. You are so very loved and missed.
thank you to all our family and friends who helped make today a little less sad and a lot more full of happiness

10/18/14

Rain

What a nice day for rain
Think my dad had some tears for us today
At the same time giving us what we need ♡
Love u dad
This happened for kid's party too

10/31/14

10 months without you

I know you do not want me to cry
You never ever have
You always told me how strong I am
You always rushed to me if I was ever in any pain
You were always there to bring my smile back.
Today makes 10 months that both you and heaven
decided it was time
Although I am happy you are no longer in pain
I can't seem to stop these tears from falling from my face
I can't fill the emptiness in my soul
I lost a huge piece of who I am
I look through your pictures, look back on memories,

hear your voice in my head
And I'm still learning from your patience, your love, your realness,

I'm still learning from your authenticity
No one will ever be all you were to me, for us
Your irreplaceable
forever loved and missed
My dad. Forever and always. Always and forever.

11/21/14

it will be 10 months this month
it's been a long expensive, stressful road to get your headstone done
but i just heard back from the cemetery
"The stone is in transit from the factory and will be here late this week."
crossing fingers, so many holidays and things have passed with this not yet done
I am ready for it to be complete.
hopefully all is perfect
and your happy and proud.

11 months without you

11 months ago I had to say my hardest goodbye
It still feels like yesterday
I showed you cell phone pictures of the kids until they arrived
That kept you here , they're why you stayed
You lived for me, for us
I wanted you to live, to fight your hardest to stay and not give up
I wanted you to know if you felt it was time to move on, that was ok-you had been through more than enough
I told you id fight for you and I did
Even though you're not here, your memories live
Not a day goes by that I don't cry
That I don't wish for your life
But not a day goes by that my love for you doesn't grow
Not a day goes by....I know, you know
I love you dad

12/21/14

Headstone, finally

got the email today that your headstone has made it to your resting spot finally after 11months.
This has been the hardest 11months ever.
No day has been easy
I miss you every day, I love you, I'll be making a visit very soon.
For 11months I've been waiting for this part of the process to be complete.
I pray its perfect. You deserve it.
Holy sepulchre cemetery. .....

12/26/14

21 days before

exactly 1 year ago we celebrated 2 hours at round table for New Year's Eve with angel and his other half of his family. you were so tired and sick I remember telling you to stay home and rest and not to push yourself too hard and you said 'if I couldn't do it I wouldn't" there's was no place you'd rather be. you wanted every last moment with us and to enjoy every last holiday and second. you wouldnt stop smiling even while in pain and falling asleep. 1 year ago we took one of our last pictures, 1 of my all-time favorites.
who knew 21 days later heaven and you would meet.
I remember last year saying everything is perfect because I still had you, I had everything that meant everything to me and that's all that mattered
anytime together was my favorite days
this year has been the hardest year of my life because it has been a year of firsts without you.
today we celebrate this day and it's the first without you, you're not waking up with us for 2015 but your forever in my heart and forever a big part of me, I love you dad.

12/31/14

12 months without you

1 year ago today I had to be the strongest I could ever be while feeling the worst pain I have ever felt.
January 21,2014 at 12:40pm my father told me he was done with the machines. He was ready to be taken off and end the battle with liver cancer.
You could see the fear and sadness and pain in his eyes, you could hear the faith and certainty in his voice.
On this day last year we faced the day, the moment-we never wanted to come.
The inevitable point in life
On that day I not only had to say goodbye but I had to see my children say goodbye with not understanding why or what it meant.
This has easily been the hardest year ever.
Of life without an important piece of my life, heart and soul missing
A year of firsts - holidays, birthdays, days without him.
A first year of the rest of what life will now be.
Digital frames, blankets, altar, memories, t-shirts and such all-around for comfort, for remembrance.
.....last year I made hundreds of shirts and passed them out in his memory.

Please if you have one, put it on. Share his smile and stories with the world. Help me, help him touch lives and forever live on.

If you don't have a shirt, raiders or A's will do.

I'm in the process of making buttons.

"Don't thank me, thank GOD" he'd say and I would reply "I thank him every day for you"

it's been 1 year since you've been gone and yet your still very much alive.

I want to say thank you for tonight. I was so nervous, excited, feeling unknown about today because to me today is not a day for celebration or for sadness but yet it was both.

Tonight, I had a dessert table made in honor and remembrance of my dad. Family came over for dinner and time together. We spent time and enjoyed each other's company. We shared stories about my dad. A room full of people wearing shirts with his face and smile on them.

1/21/15

Sometimes

Sometimes I feel like I could say I miss you and the whole world would hear/feel how powerful it is that the universe would give you back to me,
like heaven would feel my pain and just send you back to me.
Every day while we eat at the table, we have the digital frame playing. It is a frame that plays with many pictures of you.
Every day I cry-I try not to let anyone see.
Sometimes I just feel like this love could be felt strong enough for you to walk out of a picture.
why can't it be like a movie?
why can't your spirit be seen and heard?
dad, we all miss and love you so much.
It feels like everyone says the first year is the hardest. The first year of firsts without you.
Hardest barley describes it.
heartbreak is just a little of it.
As thankful as I am for everything-I can't help but breakdown.
I can't help wanting to scream at the sky for you to come back...........
everyday seems to be-just 1 of those days ☺

7/27/14

First year without you

There was so much more I wanted and could've done yesterday to mark your 1 year. Instead I didn't stress myself. I went with the flow, the things that didn't happen did not cause me any feelings.

I'm thankful with life, for time, for patience, for all the love and support.

If anything, yesterday made me want to have more family dinners just because,

I sat and enjoyed what I heard and saw.

I didn't take a tun if photos, I was too busy enjoying the moment and soaking in the words, laughter, visuals. It was a blessed day/night.

I'm going to make a conscious effort to live everyday like that, stress-free, in the moment.

Thank you dad for your memories, bringing us together and all you taught and gave so many. I love u

Things change quickly

It's been a little over a year since you left.
yesterday I was so sick,
I felt so horrible
almost like I needed to go to the hospital,
I was sleeping so much---part of me thought with how
bad I felt that I would see you somehow-
in my dreams, in whatever sign, but I could feel that
possibility so much right now.
I felt like being that sick or tired would somehow bring
you closer to me, it would bring us closer together
Do I sound crazy? Am I crazy to feel this way? Would it
make anything better?
today, the buttons I have been waiting on arrived
I opened the box and past so many out in no time.
This is another way to share your smile and story
This is another way to see love and support surrounding me.
It is another gesture to show my love for you
It is another way those who love you can share their love
for you.
Those last few days of your life were full of blood,
needles, doctors and noisy machines,
you were having trouble breathing, you were crying,
you were in pain if anyone touched your legs or feet,

you were swollen and there was no way for release,
your liver wasn't functioning properly
it couldn't get any better, unfortunately.
I kept trying to keep you warm because I knew you were always cold
It was so hard to keep you warm, hospitals are so cold.
Every time you closed your eyes id cry and beg for them to open again
never knowing when it would be the last time, not wanting the end.
Doctors were telling me for days this was it, it was over and it was time to say goodbye
And I said you do what you can to save him, it's not over, he's moving, he's fighting, its not his time.
I would tell them "he's here, he's not gone."
Part of me felt bad for putting you through so much.
I put you through so much to keep you here
I felt selfish and the other part of me felt horrible agreeing with you to be taken off of machines, like I should have fought harder.
Agreeing to take you off of those machines felt like I was giving up
I know you said it was what you wanted, but was it really you want?
I'd never give up on you-id fight for you forever
Do you feel like I gave up on you? Cause I would, never.

While you were ok-you had told me if machines were ever keeping you alive that I'd have to be strong and take you off.

It's so different when its real. I just wanted time to stop. The doctors told me the machines were keeping you alive, that if they turned them off, you would last only minutes

I was hearing them and part of me didn't want to believe it.

I remember having to make that first call to family having to actually say you were leaving us and soon, I could barely speak while crying.

I could barely say it and I had to keep calling more and more people

because you deserved all your loved ones there with you. the doctors said only a few people but we were a crowded room and waiting room

people all in the halls and people still on their way to you.

you greeted people by name as they came in, you laughed, you smiled, you prayed

---I thought that meant you'd be ok, that you would stay. Every piece of you fought to stay

I knew it couldn't be easy to make the choice to go away.

I told myself if you survived off the machines then you weren't as sick as the doctors thought

Healing While Hurting

but once the machines went off, it wasn't long.
My heart was racing and my eyes were looking everywhere fast
I was checking numbers, looking at your chest, holding your hand-knowing the time wasn't going to last.
It wasn't long until you closed your eyes for the last time
I saw all of the pain leave your face; I knew right at that time.
your voice, your smile-it was all gone-just like that
not a day goes by that I don't miss you and love you more than I ever have.
Not a day goes by that the kids don't ask for you
that we don't talk about you, that we don't cry missing you.
cancer didn't win that day
cancer made life harder but it never defined or crippled your spirit, even on your worst days.
I love you dad
forever and always, always and forever

1/29/15

That day is still today

It feels all too real like that day
every time I close my eyes, I'm back at that hospital
having to let go and walk away.
it's hard
Constant tears and headaches, with a broken heart.
dad I can't say I miss and love you enough
You were my run to when I was alone, when I needed to vent or feel loved.
you were the true definition of "one call away"
You don't know how many times this past year I wanted to call and text you missing your face.
I miss your voice
Needing your words, heart, patience, faith-opinions when I can't make a choice.
I'll never stop missing you
You'll never ever be forgotten by any of us.
you are Truly one of a kind
Life is definitely a crazy beautiful ride
I didn't know, and still don't know how Wednesday is going to hit me
But I knew I'd need and want the day off because I know it will get to me.
Its almost a year since you've been gone

I don't think you know, until you know-this feeling of missing someone.
A year of eating my meals with a digital frame of you
A year of writing on Facebook as if I was talking to you.
Today I looked at my keychains in the store and broke out in tears
Missing you is hard on my heart, the pictures don't replace you being here.
Remembering you is easy, it's both painful and comforting
I love you is easy, I guess healing is through the hurting.
I can't believe how much time has passed
A blanket of you hangs on our wall and it's like you're here watching us.
The kids have blankets and bears with photos of you and that has to be good enough
Those items have to be good enough to wipe tears and to hug.
Not a day has passed that we don't speak of you, cry for you and wish you were still here
I love you dad, we love you- sometimes pain brings fear.

1/19/15

Bad dream

I had a dream of you last night
It's been a long time since I have
I don't remember all the details
I just remember you hugging me and tears falling like a waterfall, me not wanting you to go
......my dad, my superhero, my motivation, my peacemaker, my mirror, my soul......
The moment you decided to let go, I responded with its going to be ok, I respect your choice, we had no choice but to face our biggest fear
I remember all my thoughts, my tears, my hopes
Hoping when they turned the machines off that you'd survive
Praying every time you closed your eyes that you'd open them again
It felt so unreal leaving your side knowing you weren't ever going to be leaving with me again
Its still all too real, life changing for sure-to say the least
I miss you dad. I love you. every day is a struggle. And every day I am thankful, grateful for the memories, for the no more suffering, for the times that are easier than others and for the love that continues to grow.

1/18/15

The day is getting closer

I know the day is getting closer
The feelings are becoming too much
The headaches are intense
Breathing is a bit harder
Tears are more
.....January 21,2014 I saw you take your last breath
Heard you say you love me for the last time
Felt your hand let me go
Felt your body lose warmth
Saw the pain leave your face
....it's almost been a year and the memories, those last few days, those first couple months, this whole first year has been a wound that's still too fresh
Sometimes I still don't believe it
Sometimes I still ask why
....I miss you dad. I love you.

1/17/15

Relating everything back to you

Every day I spend a lot of time thinking of you
relating everything back to you.
"my dad would like that" "my dad use to love that" "i remember" "i wish"
I still cry thinking of you---almost a week away from a year since you've been gone and the tears are just starting to become not an everyday basis.
I think of how you'd wake up and never leave your bed a mess, it had to be fixed/tucked perfectly
Wow, That's also so me.
you had so much patience
you'd wash dishes even when it looked as though you couldn't stand or hold a dish.
you'd spend your last penny on anything we needed or wanted
you'd say grace every time we ate and we all always loved it.
I miss seeing you in your chair, watching you watch tv
you loved your music, you loved your movies, you were very protective and yet so giving.
if a man asked to wash your windows on your car-you would say yes and you'd even get out and help him
You would start conversation and over pay him.
you loved to help anyone

you'd even give change to those begging who you knew were going to get beer, you didn't judge.
-you'd say "I've been there"
you'd pass on the word of how you changed, your story and hope to touch other's.
I miss you all the time, you know how much I loved and love you
I know you still know- all cant be felt with the truth.
I can't believe that even with you gone-the love still grows
It's a feeling you have to feel in order to really know.
not a single day goes by that I don't have flashbacks
that I don't have what if's, what is this? What if that?
Not a day goes by that I don't have pain
that I still can't believe I won't see you here again.
I love you dad-always and forever-forever and always

1/13/15

2 years without you

I can't imagine the words you'd say.....
Or I guess, it hurts more- because, I can only imagine what you'd say.
These past two years you've been gone so much has happened
You'd be so proud and happy, I know you are in heaven.
We have our own place, the kids are taking classes for their first communion
I'm taking classes to get baptized, I ended one job and started another closer to home.
Edgardo got his license, I got my permit again
many babies have been born; some family members are fighting battles in silence.
Edgardo is doing good not drinking, we are going to the gym
birthdays holidays-all those usual celebrations we celebrate with you on a blanket.
in 34 days we are getting married through church for our convalidation....
without you it will be so hard, I can and can't imagine.
I know you'd be happy that this time angel will be a part of this special day

How do I picture walking down any isle without you,
how do I picture a fatherless father daughter dance, it won't be the same.
All I can do is be thankful 6 years ago you were there for it all
and that in 34 days we will have made it to a goal we once talked about with you.
The goals do not stop there
many more goals to accomplish still.

1/25/16

Church

A beautiful Sunday, Angel Normally doesn't sit with us at church but today he got to Today mass was dedicated to you.
The children heard your name mentioned a couple of times and looked at me
Hearing your name instantly had tears rolling down my cheeks.
We enjoyed this rare moment for us
Thankful, even though it was extremely hard for us all.

1/24/16

Every day is a struggle

Every day is a struggle, a challenge, a dealing process
Its true holidays and events sometimes hit harder-but every day has its feelings to deal with.
I've known tomorrow makes two years but it's truly hitting me now
It truly hurts so much, time doesn't matter -even now.
The world was a better place with you in it. My heart was complete with you here
My world was perfect as it could be. But tomorrow makes two years.
Two years that your fight with liver cancer ended and I still can't control the tears
I still want to call you because I could tell you any and everything and I have so much for you to hear.
There's no shirts, pictures, buttons, digital frames or memories that can take the place of having you here
Losing you is a pain that can't be totally accepted or even healed.
The only grandpa my children had and the best at that
The only dad a girl can ever need, the one I got to have.
I was lucky to be your daughter

I was blessed to have you as my father.
Life will never be life, like it was with you dad
Miss you always, love you forever. This process is hard to understand.

1/20/16

I could write a book

I could write a book on what a great man, person, friend, grandfather, father-in-law, worker and dad you were and will forever be
I could write a million different posts of beautiful memories.
Your honesty was always too honest until you got sick and didn't know how to tell me things knowing it would hurt
Your heart was so huge, you were always doing for others even when you should have been taking care of you.
You gave even what you didn't have to give
Your smile will forever be a million-dollar smile, that you passed on to me and the kids.
you smiled and laughed so much that most didn't know the horrendous pain you were in 3 years battling cancer
Every time you went to the hospital doctors were amazed you were still here.
Every Christmas you would make your rounds surprising so many families and children with gifts
You loved to eat- especially when I cooked, I haven't cooked the same since.
You loved me and your grandkids so much that you put us first, last and everywhere in between

Those who were there the day you passed-know exactly what this means.
those last moments of your life, you stayed waiting for the kids
it was only until you got to say goodbye to them that you let go and went to heaven.
Were you perfect? No but to me yes-
clean and sober for a decade and that couldn't be easy, especially when dealing with cancer stress.
you tried to help others as well
There's so much I could say and share.
so much the world is missing out on
so much I feel honored to be a part of
and yet sad that there's not more to add
But you live on through me, memories and your grandkids.
It hurts bad.
but I am well aware how blessed I am.
Moments in time fill my head, tears fill my eyes and love fills my broken heart
you continue to impact even while away, whether near or far.
As I sit in my tears, I truly can't help myself
not only did the world lose someone so amazing, unlike anyone else.
but my children lost their only grandpa

they still ask when is he coming back and talk about how much they miss him.

Two years ago, my heart broke and hasn't been able to feel complete ever since

My world hasn't been the same, my life is missing a huge piece and its you dad.

It's not like a holiday or birthday missing you

Today I feel all the pain of those last moments and days with you, this is year two.

the pain is very much real

I can't wait for a moment today to cry it out so I can be the strong person I usually am.

I want to celebrate your life, love and beautiful memories you left behind

Two years ago we spoke our last words, gave our last hugs and watched you go to the next life.

And the pain just doesn't go away.

1/21/16

3 years without you

There's a part of me that still questions it all
You were greeting people.
you were talking-how did you not get better?
Some part of me doesn't fully trust the doctors.
I still question how you weren't able to survive without machines
I still question if I should've pushed the fight for life or if I did the right thing.
yes, I remember. I remember how tired you looked
I remember the talks when you were great telling me you never wanted to survive by a machine, I remember the pain you were in not being able to use the restroom.
I remember you unable to spit, eat or drink
I remember the look in your eyes and face, I remember the feelings.
And I remember your last breath and how I waited thinking, no it can't be real
and I waited for you to open your eyes again but they would not and loss was all I could feel.
I remember your face was at peace and my heart was in pieces
I had to leave without you and I was praying for different.
Today makes 3 years but tears fall as if I'm living that day

My heart breaks the same.
Three years later, it's not any easier
Especially with 3 kids who miss their grandpa constantly
and me, just a girl who wants her dad back.

3 years grieving

Originally, we thought we'd go to nations and have my
dad's favorite breakfast:
3egger, French toast, half bacon half sausage that he'd
share with all the kids.
But instead I cooked breakfast for the house
my mom joined late, we all put our shirts on for my dad.
My dad loved left overs with a fried egg on it
He'd prefer a Home cooked meal by me over going out
to eat, so that's what we did.
So here's how we honor him today.
3 years ago I lost a piece of my heart
I would've rather have gladly given up a piece of my liver
if it meant not having to live out this part.
but my dad would not allow it
and I had to respect it.
3years ago my dad couldn't eat or drink,
he was suffering.
he spoke, smiled, laughed and prayed with us all
before letting go at 12:40.
3years later and the pain is just as painful
I love and miss you all the time, that's the journey for me.
We don't come here to the cemetery often to visit
I feel most connected to my dad at home and at church,
I pictured that different.

I don't feel most connected here at the Cemetery
Or maybe it hurts too much, maybe its too real for me.
I know when my dad was alive he'd talk about how he didn't visit the Cemetery enough (his sister, mom, family) and he'd always say how he wanted to visit more-to put fresh flowers, say a prayer and clean the headstones up.
So I know it means a lot to him when we make time to visit
I know it means a lot to him to add flowers, say a prayer and sit with him.
His resting spot is between statues, a baseball field and hills with animals roaming
It's perfect Because he loved hearing the kids, going to baseball games/playing watching.
he was spiritual and loved life
hi dad. We're here, even if not for too long, we made the time.
It's cold and it's wet; Not that you're not worth being in the cold for
I guess it's all excuses, to leave and not stay longer.
Every time we come, your spot is emptier than we left it we continue to add to it.
A beautiful walk just us three
New books and hot chocolate for Iris and Angels' recent achievements.
They talked about what they miss most about grandpa "his hugs"

"He was everyone's grandpa, the neighbors and anyone"
but he was ours.
He didn't leave anyone out"

1/21/17

4 years without you

Once again, we made plans today. To wake up at 6:30 and get to the cemetery by 7:30 and church by 9. But as I was up by 6, I couldn't see those plans happening. I know it would have to be done at that timing so that angel could be a part of it. I know we have no problem waking up early.

But I decided let the kids sleep, it's freezing outside. Instead we got up at 8. I'm feeling very emotional. The tears won't stop.

There's so many things going on with people I love and with my dad on my heart, I'm just lost and stuck.

4 years ago today I lost the best father a girl could have, best father in law a husband could have, best grandpa any kid could ask for.

Heartbroken still. It's like this wound never heals.

1/16/18

It may seem crazy that I write the times of things happening. It may seem crazy the details I keep. I share my journey in the most honest way I can. I share because I want to remember the facts. I share to let you know its ok to be true to you. Its ok to heal however you need to. This is how I heal.

Carolina Ayala

Going back to that day, again

January 20, 2014 was one of the hardest days ever. My life definitely changed.

When my mom called me saying my dad wouldn't wake up and me running my fastest against the sirens of the ambulance. Leaving my kids without many words why. Hours at hospitals in fear and pain and tiredness. I was losing him and yet thinking he would pull through. This was just the beginning of the hardest days ever.

I spent this morning, 4 years later -still saying why didn't I see he needed help sooner? He had gone to bed earlier than normal the night before, he didn't want to get up to go eat with us, he wasn't as talkative and he was tired. Why did I think he just needed rest? Why didn't I insist he go with us on our trip a couple days earlier? I put him through a lot this day trying to save him and not lose him. It's 4 years later, this still feels like yesterday. Tears fall so easy. I miss you daily. I pray for you daily, wish for you, talk to you.

Today is hard. 4 years later. The kids are now 11,10, 6 and one on the way. Edgardo (my husband) is so much like you in all the positive ways and struggles. I am still me, a daughter that misses her father. Life would be better with you here. Thankful you are no longer suffering. I wish cancer didn't take you from us.

Today ,2018 , it's a Saturday, so we have angel and today we will celebrate your life together.

We ♡ you. Always and forever. Forever and always.

1/120/18

Breakfast and more

My dad would always get the giant 3egger... over medium eggs, French toast, half bacon half sausage.... he'd share with the kids. I'd get something with hash browns and give him half. Then he'd get several flavors of pie.

We made it here for dinner, per kids request

4 years ago, we laid you to rest. It's still hard for me to think of that day.

It was absolutely beautiful considering the reason why.

We don't visit the cemetery too much, but we will again sometime soon.

4years ago was such a hard-painful challenging beautiful day.

Miss you always dad Still grateful to all who came out that day

On Friday the kids were discussing how they want to remember/celebrate their grandpa on the 21st.

"What did he like to do?" "What's something he wanted to do" "maybe we can finish his bucket list for him"

My dad always wanted to take the boys fishing, go for a pedicure-to name a couple most talked about things and he didn't get to. I love that angel said let's finish his bucket list for him. I love that iris wants to do everything my dad loved to do. And I love that Leo wants to watch videos to remember.

1/14/18

For me, losing my dad has been very hard. For me, keeping all the details is important. Documentation is important. I don't want to forget these pieces of him. I don't want to forget our memories. I want to remember everything.
If you knew you were going to lose someone tomorrow, what would you want to remember?

Dad:

Dad: I think of you every day, although I don't write or speak every thought like I did before. I still cry, although not as much, it's still a lot. I still wish and pray and wonder and hope so many things. It's rare but you still are in some dreams.

you have always been proud of who you are, Mexican American, Apatchi. You spoke Spanglish, not Spanish very well. Your humor was not always funny, and mostly dirty adult humor. You loved the EAGLE, fast and furious movies, stingray, you had tattoos you wish you didn't, you had scars that you didn't regret, you changed your life to be clean and sober for many years, you were the sign of the cancer. You loved me and your grandchildren. you loved all children and people, you helped those who many would say didn't deserve your help. When people would beg for change , you gave it even if you knew or thought the person was going to use it for drugs or alcohol and you would tell me "that use to be me, everyone has to learn on their own time." you always wanted to take the boys fishing, we made it to Disneyland. You would buy a car or rent a place big enough for us all to fit if we wanted. You were very proud of your job at Connolly's. you made friends everywhere and you never turned your back on family.

I could go on, I miss you. I miss having you around. I miss you.

5 years without you

5 years ago, today and I cry just as hard
I still hope like a child this day wasn't real
I miss you dad
I had an idea of plans today: to have lunch at round table with angel's other family. My husband got off early. It couldn't work out with us all in the process of trying to find new homes. But what beautiful memories.
5 years ago, for New Year's we all ate at round table together to start the year off.
Then 5 years ago today we all lost you. Physically we lost you. I still don't understand why you couldn't pull through when you were so conscious and alert. But I also remember all the swelling, the pain, the tiredness. Your wishes for nature to run its course and to not let machines keep you alive. I remember all the struggle.
I remember that day. As I sit in the bathroom balling my eyes out as if it was just happening- they say time heals. So much is happening in life right now and I wish it was all calmer to honor you differently.
I love you dad. Always and forever, forever and always. My life has never been the same without you. We sure do miss you so much.

1/21/19

I had a dream of you this morning dad, I could hear my sis Nicole and husband and iris saying it was time to wake up and I just didn't want to. I didn't want to leave you. We were having such a great moment. I remember almost yelling at my husband "no, I'm talking to my dad!" But I didn't.

See you the next time you visit ♡.

1/18/19

6 years ago

6 years ago, was a heartbreaking day
It was the day I had to face the reality I never wanted to face.
The reality that I would lose my dad, That I would have to say goodbye.
and still part of me thought I could save him.
that my love for him was so strong that GOD would heal him.
That he changed his life for the better so much and this wasn't going to be the end
That he was doing better, he was gonna make it.
just days, before we had went on a trip to Sonora, he was supposed to attend but he didn't
He had too many liters drained from him; this means he had too much fluid in his stomach.
he was tired, he needed rest and This was the last opportunity for the Sonora house
We thought of not going but He wanted us to go and not be the reason we miss out.
I wanted him there, Part of me wanted to force him to go because I could see the end could be near but I didn't want to believe that and I didn't really know.
the other part of me felt he needed rest with us all out of the house

that with us gone maybe he could rest better, it would all work out.

we didn't speak of his cancer

he didn't want it on social media-or even to be brought up in daily life together.

He wanted to live as if it wasn't there

He wanted to just be seen for himself, not his sickness-that was fair.

so, we mostly kept to that.

Living life making the best of it.

I'm sure some part of him wanted us to stay, only he knew his true feelings

I feel horrible I didn't stay; I feel horrible I wasn't there those two days because that's two more days we could have had that's now missing.

I feel bad I didn't convince him to come-to see that view and place and be with us

If I knew his final days were really in front of us-it would have been different.

6 years ago, I went to the room and asked if he wanted to come eat with us

He said no. I should have known. maybe I didn't want to know. But I respected his needing to rest up.

he would always get up to go with us and say "when I can't I won't."

he wasn't speaking much. I thought he needed more rest.

he was tired. he was drained. so I tucked him in because I dint want him cold.

I was going just a few blocks away and not for long-
told him I would bring him back food.
I remember feeling helpless. all these years later I wish I stayed
but everything happens for a reason, or so they say.
at lunch my mom calls and says my dad won't wake up-
when I say I dropped everything, I mean literally. I dropped everything, to run.
those babies I love so much, I left them with their dad who was working and family who were with us.
I ran the fastest ever, beating the sounds of the ambulance.
I am screaming to the sky "don't take my dad, dad don't leave me."
I made it home to see him on the ground. I was talking to him but he wasn't responding-just looking at me.
they give him a shot to help his blood sugar and it seems to help
I feel so bad if I hurt him by asking him to please not leave me-knowing he was tired and probably ready.
I wasn't hearing any good news.
this was one of the longest days ever of watching him get put through so much.
two different hospitals.
I remember telling the doctors "keep him alive, keep him here with me."
his wishes were written "let nature run its course."

I couldn't ride in the ambulance because he was in critical condition.
I was being asked about his wishes in case he stops breathing.
sitting in ICU for what felt like forever.
to me he was getting better.
he was awake, trying to talk, trying to move the doctors away …. I just knew he was going to get better…..
but the night was long.
one of those days and nights and situations where it's not where you'd ever want to be and yet there's no place you'd rather be.
these feelings hit me strong still.
I can still smell the hospital, the blood.
I can still feel the emotions. I still question my choices.
oh, how I miss you

is it hard to be thankful at times like this? sometimes. but I was thankful to have that time, family support, opportunity to accept the journey for what it was and to be a part of it. I am thankful that years later I still am reminded I am human-and I am not ok. it is ok to not be ok. and it is ok to be ok. it was hard to learn that its ok to be ok.

1/21/20

Still in the works

I Miss you dad
How can it be almost 6 years since I was with you last.
I still get sad
When you lose a loved one ,heartache seems to last.
I will never forget those final days
I won't forget your pain.
I wanted so bad to take peace in you no longer suffering
But even today I'm still selfish because I want you here living
Holding on and letting go both held unbearable hurt
GOD has a plan for all, this one still in the works
You may be gone But the work is not done
The work still continues through all whom you love
The work still progresses through those who love you
As long as I'm alive, so are you
I miss and love you. Always and forever
Forever and always
I am thankful for poetry, for being able to write and share my feelings. I am thankful for saved photos on Facebook. I am thankful my dad's Facebook page is still available. I am thankful for all the time I had with him in my life

-1/16/20

I am so thankful for loved ones who messaged me today. I was not expecting it. Before I would ask for people to wear their shirts or buttons or say a prayer. I use to feel like I needed those kinds of things to support my healing. and I did. But today I don't feel that. although those things are great and it would be nice for loved ones to do. I didn't feel the need to ask about it or for it. I know my dad is missed and loved all the time. I know he made and continues to impact lives.

today I wanted to go to church but it didn't work out with the kid's school schedules.

today I wore my sweater with our picture and a fb status of my dad's. I have the digital frame going, a candle lit and lights on.

but today what was most meaningful was texting our two oldest kids about how much their grandpa loved them and how they kept him alive. What was most meaningful was showing Leo pictures of him and his grandpa because he was a lot younger and visual is probably better. I do get sad thinking Athena is missing out but she says "grandpa" when she sees his picture as if she knows him. I see pictures of iris and my dad at Athena's age and I can see that being Athena. I see my dad in Athena, she has his chin.

this year, this day I am more at peace with this particular healing. I have always felt like a piece of my heart is forever missing-when in reality he has always been there and never left. It's true I lost myself when this all took place and I am still on the road to being my best version of me-but finally I feel that healing taking place and that transformation ready to take form.

they say time heals all. I will always hurt. there is no bandage for this wound and no eraser to take away what was. but there is gratitude and that has given me so much more. gratitude is healing me. I am thankful for that. I am thankful for new found peace with the reality and I am thankful for growth.

it took so much over every day of these last 6 years to get to this point. it shifted for me near the end of last year and I know it's here to stay because I have never been able to have a day like today in the past years since his passing.

Today was different. and I am ok with it. I am ok with healing, and I am ok with the parts that still hurt.

I love you dad. thank you for the parts of me that are you.

today I am thankful for photos and memories triggered. I am thankful for photos and the reminders. Reminders of things that aren't always at the front of the brain. Reminders of memories that are sometimes overshadowed by pain.

my dad always included everyone. If we went anywhere and I asked if so and so could join-he welcomed with open arms. If I didn't ask for others to join, he was asking.

He would spend his hard earnings on spoiling the kids, and me "you can't take it with you so I spend it while I'm here."

like many, he loved to eat. We loved breakfast at nations and their pies. We loved pigging out at Denny's. He loved "fish and chips" at foster freeze followed by an ice cream cone-chocolate dipped. He loved bacon hot dogs at the stadium with everything on them.

He always wore a watch, he had several. He always wore a big ring, he had several. He always had on a necklace of meaning; he had several. You would catch him wearing glasses often of some sort. He loved getting his hair cut and shaving and taking care of himself.

He had this comb he kept in his pocket that would go over your finger-to keep him and the boys looking sharp. A true RAIDERs fan. and A's.

into Aztec culture, artwork, history.

he loved dressing up and dressing comfortable. He loved the "dickies" brand.

He was the one I would let treat the kids to McDonalds every now and then, that was their thing.

He was there to buy my wedding dress, take me to get my belly pierced and sign the parental release. He was there to be a witness to our marriage and sign.
these are just some memories I am grateful for.
my dad loved me and his grandkids so much. the day he passed away-today, 6 years ago.... he waited for all 3 of his grandkids to make it before saying goodbye. they literally kept him holding on, kept him alive. He couldn't leave peacefully or completely without them. How much strength that must have taken, what amazing love that is.
I am thankful for him being my dad and being their grandpa and being my husband's father-in-law.
I am thankful we all got to give him that cross-over to the other side and that he gave that to us.
today is one of the first years I can say it's gotten easier. In the sense that the good outweighs the sad.
no doubt I still cry and have moments of complete hurt-confusion even. But today, today I am happy for life and the good times we had.
love you dad Juan Ayala always and forever.
forever and always

1/21/20

Healing While Hurting

On our walk home Leo said "I wish grandpa never died. Because I miss him.....he didn't want to die, he wanted to stay here with us"
This came out of nowhere, he was crying as we were walking in the heat home...something triggered that thought

9/7/16

10.29.20 illustration
By
Leonardo Juan-Edgar Velasquez

Another last

I just want another last,
Another last text and call
Another last conversation
Another picture together
Another holiday or day together
Another last hug and smile
Another last movie and meal
Another last accomplishment and victory
Another last goodnight and good morning
I just want another last
Anything with you so that the past isn't just the past
I just want another tomorrow
You just can't be gone, we had so many plans for our tomorrows
I just want to hear your voice again
Hold my hand again
We had great times but I guess I'm greedy,I want more
Just one more last, I'll always want just one more

3/19/14

Say It

Hard for him to say, hard for me to hear
Easy flow of tears
My dad telling me that when the day comes
If he's on life support-that I have to be strong
And I will have to tell them to let him go
Because at that point, it will be my say so
Not an easy reality to think of
Lately he has been having so much done
Liver cancer has been a hard journey
He just had 5 liters of fluid drained to help with bloating and swelling
They have to re-do the surgery from before that caused his bleeding
They still have to do even more draining
My dad used to say he would never get cancer because that's his zodiac sign
He has survived so much in his life
It kills us all to know he is going through this
Let's stay hopeful because I can't stand the thought of losing him
He is a fighter and I believe there is always hope
This conversation was unexpected but I am so thankful he let me know

12/26/13

Grieving

There were days I was grieving you before you left this earth,
Even before we knew you had cancer.

When we didn't live together, I would often think "is this how it will all be?"
But it's completely different not living together vs not living.

You would ask me to move in but I felt like my mom needed me
Id ask myself "would I regret it if God took you from me?"

In the end I didn't want to regret not living with you,
I wanted to be there even if it was hard to do.
When you got sick is when we made that shift,
It was at the end but at the time, we didn't know it.

I wanted to be there, even if it was hard to see
And it was hard, hard doesn't even describe it for me.
It was unbearable to see
All the pain, all the suffering.
Seeing all the support you needed
And knowing you had been doing it alone when I should have known I was needed.

I hadn't really been there to see
I hadn't been there to help to the best of my ability.

As a parent, you wanted to protect me,
You wanted to shield me.
You were scared too,
You needed me as much as I needed you.

Before you left earth, I was already trying to cope,
Sometimes I lost hope.
I was in denial,
I pretended for a while.
I pretended your diagnosis wasn't real,
I prayed for a miracle and that you would heal.

Sometimes I would bring the hard stuff up,
Through messenger or text because to say it was sometimes too tough.
Through messenger I could say I tried,
Whether or not you gave a reply

I still write you on Facebook sometimes…….

9/19/20

Even in the end I remember telling myself "what's meant to be will be"

You will keep breathing on your own, or the doctors will be right about the machines

I was trying to convince myself,
Truth is, it didn't help

Process to progress

For so long I would keep track of the days, months and then years
I would write to you on Facebook, as if you were here
I had your Facebook password but I only posted once after you passed
Just to update your friends and people, that I knew I didn't have
I can never say to anyone "I know what you are going through"
I only know how I have felt and feel, I only know my truth
I can't say "I know how you feel" because I don't
Sometimes I feel I can relate but grief is a slippery slope
I can share my journey and hope it helps
For me, I know how this has felt
But my process is just mine
Everyone goes through grief in their own ways and own time.

9/12/20

Different

I knew when you left life would be different but I didn't know how different it'd make me.
I knew when you left I'd be heartbroken but heartbroken doesn't describe the pain I'm feeling.
I knew I'd still have so much to say even though I held nothing back.
I knew I'd regret some choices even though I said I wouldn't while making them.
You left and a piece of me left with you.
A part of me died too.
Every day I cry even though I know it changes nothing.
Every day I try to smile but it hurts when I find myself smiling.
Pictures just aren't enough even though I love that I have so many.
Videos are wonderful but everything is just a memory.
A new liver was what you needed because cancer was not letting it work properly.
You were all we needed because you made us more than happy.
I knew when you left life would be different
I just didn't know how different it'd make me

4/14/14

Never really gone

I just want you to know the day you left me and all of
us-you did not leave alone
a part of me, a huge part of me left with you
and the best parts of you stayed with me, live in me
dad you'll never be gone, not really, not spiritually
so many hospital visits people would say what if this is it?
what if something goes wrong? what if?
so many hospital visits I was there by your side because
although each and every time it was the hardest to see-I
couldn't imagine not being there for you
it kills me every day to think you knew you were leaving-
imagining what that must feel like to know you're going
to die
it kills me every day because although you were strong
and accepting-i could still see the sadness and pain and
tears in your eyes
all I wanted to do was stay by that hospital bed until your
eyes opened again
all I wanted to do was stay until I could see you
breathing again
all I wanted to do was stay with you, keep you warm and
comfortable and at peace
all I wanted was to save you from cancer, from death,
from pain and from any sad/bad feelings

the day you left me almost 4 months ago still feels like just yesterday
some days I still feel like you'll call or knock on the door or hug me-some days I just want to see you and tell me its ok
the day you left me-a piece of my heart and soul went missing
my smile was lost, my fears became real and everything became heartbreaking
I use to be ok at goodbyes-I accepted reality
I use to be ok with life knowing death happens until it took you from me

5/19/14

Picture memories

my pictures of us together are now ones from the past
Ones from the cemetery
I could sit here all day and make memories last
Sit here with a bracelet and shirt that says in memory
I use to come here with you to visit your mom and
grandma and talk to your sister, rest in peace
Now I come here with my loved ones to talk to you
about all our family
Leo is so excited saying I'm going to see my grandpa!
And he's only 3 it's hard to explain and tell him where is
grandpa
But we are here dad, tears in my eyes, on my cheeks,
We are here this memorial day sharing memories
I love you, I miss you, we all do
And it hurts so much more cause I know you miss being
here with us too

5/26/14

Always and never

I wish heaven would send you back to me
Heaven better celebrate father's day in all the ways I
never could and in every way i did
Heaven is lucky to have you
And I thank GOD for the time he gave us
Of course I still ask why
I'm thankful you're not in pain
I'm angry I couldn't save you
And really I just miss you
I'm missing a piece of my heart
I'll never fully recover

6/14/14

Part of me

a part of me died with you and a part of me lives for you
I love you dad. I miss you
I'm forever incomplete, I'll be forever missing a piece of my heart
But I'm forever grateful and thankful

Taking over me

that was definitely you taking over me. Only you would still give to those who hurt us. Only you would beg me to forgive when I feel I can't and don't want to. You would give no matter how much I tried to convince you it wasn't right.

I just gave to the one person who's brought me so much pain, trauma, drama and stress. Somebody who deserves their own karma and didn't deserve a gift, especially from me.

And yet I did it all while wondering what's come over me. this gift changes nothing.

It's you dad. That was you taking over me. I realized it had to be you and I'll let it be as that.it is what it is and I can hear your voice still and I know your real proud and happy.

6/25/14

On the lake

My dad's family paid for us to take a train trip to visit them and get to know them for a few days. I am not one to ever go out of my comfort zone like this but we decided to do it.

This is just a post from one of many moments:

A great 8 hours at don Padro lake... the kids did not want to try jet skis but then did not want to leave or get off of them....it was so wonderful being with family. right when we got on the water my husband points in the sky and I look and smile. Iris screams it's an eagle its grandpas' favorite bird!!! On the way leaving angel says I wish grandpa could have come with us...all I can say is he was there, oh yes, the whole time... love you dad...I'm sure the kids are dreaming of you because angel never falls asleep so quickly, they are all passed out

I know you are here with us, not just on my bracelet or mind. I had a good cry on the train thinking of you. The kids brought you up a lot today in terms of this trip. They say your brother (Everette) reminds them of you.... they have a turtle here and right away the kids thought it was one of yours. Your pictures are on the walls. Its nice. It's a nice feeling to be here.

Our first stop was panda express (only I got food here) can you believe a whole stop just for me, everyone else got burger king. I'm not use to not paying or to having people really think of me, of us. like the kids say-thank you grandpa for family and like you say don't thank me, thank GOD. I thank you both. Love you. Goodnight

6/27/14

Everytime

every time I think positive and find a piece of peace in
the reality, the sadness takes over in no time
Those last 3days of seeing you suffer, fight and go haunts
my mind
I miss you all the time, there's nothing that can change that
I cry all the time, there's nothing that can stop that
A piece of my heart and soul will forever be gone, there's
no healing that
I love you dad

7/15/14

I Hope You Knew

I just want you to know, everything I hope you already knew,
everything I know you know.... that I love you.
my tears of missing you aren't because I'm not strong,
they are just because I love you so much.
life without you is incomplete
but that does not mean I am not grateful for the time and memories.
My tears don't mean I live in regret
 but I can't help but wish for you back and wish things could have been different.
I wish the day of the funeral wasn't so sad for me
because i would have loved to actually spend time with all the people who came together for you and our family.
Many days I still can't believe all of this isn't a bad dream,
I sometimes forget I won't be hearing your voice,
answering your call, seeing your face-in person and this reality.
sometimes I still forget you're not here
I know its selfish to wish you were still here.
I know you were in pain but I know how much you loved us and life
and i know you'd never leave us if you didn't feel it was time.

I know you trusted GOD
I know in the end you were at peace with it all.
I know you were not ready to go
At the same time, you were ready to go.
part of me will always think I should have fought harder
that somehow, I could have saved you- if only I tried harder.
I know when it comes to cancer-it plays out how it does
there's really nothing any of us can do
except make the best of the worst thing
I love you dad, I miss you……
pictures, videos and memories
just aren't enough even though they have to be

7/24/14

Convinced?

caught in a moment
tears falling again, it feels constant
I just remember saying please don't give up
you said let this run its course, GOD will say when time is up
you kept telling me either way you win
you said here you win and when you leave you win
sometimes I wasn't sure who you were trying to convince
I know you truly believed it
but I know no matter what you'd rather stay
and at the same time you didn't deserve to stay-not with so much pain
every day you had a smile on your face
even when the angels took your breath away
I held you until your body got colder
I know life isn't fair but I'm still daddy's little girl
the grown up part of me accepts death as a part of life
but the daughter in me wants to scream at heaven and
tell them they can't have you because you're mine
if I could fight for you I would fight the battle
you fought the best anyone could-so many didn't even know your struggle
cancer made so much in life harder

in the end heaven gained another
but cancer does not win, it will not ever
I believe everything makes us better
not 1 day goes by that I don't want to rewind time
not 1 day goes by that tears don't fill my eyes
not 1 day goes by that I can find the missing piece of my heart
forever I'll be incomplete without you

7/29/14

Rebuild

some heartbreaking things broke my heart
with all that was good I was still falling apart
I couldn't find a fix for the wrong that happened
I couldn't heal from what happened
things started to rebuild
little pieces started to heal
I continued to grow
I had you-that helped me the most
knowing I had you here made me feel like I would be alright
having you in this same house, even when I left I knew you were always by my side
even while you were here I carried you so heavy in my heart
then one day you left-to be a part of the stars
then I had a new heartbreak
a new heartache
and it doesn't heal right without you
it will never heal without you
and those parts of me that got better, seemed to be back at square one
I lost you and I lost me too and it can't be undone
you gave me strength, smiles, hope, peace
losing you to the afterlife stole so many things

but memories are forever
love is forever
I still have such a long life to live
the way I feel for you, I hope I mean to my kids
and if I do then I know I have to continue to do better
because they need me and I have to find closure
I'll keep you alive for me, for them , for you
it'll never be the same but life is what we make it-I know
that to be true
....dad I love you
love you dad. This is going to be a tough month and yet
it's also going to be beautiful in so many ways-I'm sure I
can't even yet imagine

9/15/14 and 1/27/14

Carolina Ayala

Remembering is my favorite gift that also hurts

dad....

There's so many days I try not to cry but it only makes me cry more

So many times I just want to call you, just once more

You were always there, just a call away

Always there to dry the tears on my face

I get it, i get that we will all die one day

I get it, this is life, but it doesn't help the pain

It hurts way too much knowing I can't hold your hand

I can't have your hug or a forehead kiss from my dad

It hurts way to much visioning you walking by my side

Imagining your spirit, accepting you're not alive

You get brought up often and poor Leo thinks you've been at the doctors all this time

Going on 11months without you and he thinks you're getting better with time

Remembering conversations keeps me positive

Remembering can hurt so much but it's also my favorite gift

12/13/14

Holding your hand

I remember holding your hand while you laid in the hospital bed
Every time your eyes closed id beg you to open them
So scared every second
Not knowing what would be the last moment
But knowing it was coming
Doctors saying you were going
I remember telling you to please not leave me
I remember yelling to the sky to not take you from me
I remember touching your hair, telling myself to never forget
I remember looking in your eyes-letting the eyes say what the mouth couldn't
Sometimes there's no words
And yet we both heard
I remember watching the pain leave your face
And I'll never forget all that took place those last days
Because it still feels like yesterday
And I can't seem to end the pain to this day

12/9/14

We don't have forever

we knew we didn't have forever
we knew you had cancer
we knew you had pain
everyone always saw a smile on your face
tears when we talked about not making it to forever
smiles when we talked about our memories together
.....we lived life knowing what you were diagnosed with
but keeping it private because you didn't want people to
treat you different
you didn't want any fake-ness
you just wanted to live as happy as you could with the
people who were always consistent
.....although I took so many pictures and never changed
because of cancer
I now wish we could have been more intentional
like with book and videos
we both knew how much you'd be missed by me and the
kids
I wish we were more intentional of the reality of what
missing you would be like
I wish we had videos of certain things you'd say
the jokes, the songs, your laugh, the way you'd say our
names

I wish we had boos, letters, notes -intentionally to us
I wish we would have done all that but some things you
don't think of until it's over and done
so we work with what's left-snippets, pictures, memories
I'll keep you alive forever-forever you are a part of we

9/9/14

Since you passed

last night as the longest dream I've had of you since you've passed away.

I have had a few that seem like appearances, short visits.

But last night was all night, even when I woke up I was able to go right back to where I left off.

This dream was more normal in ways, you were living with us. I was able to check on you in your room like i often did and ask you what you needed or wanted.id ask are you hungry? what do you want to eat? you'd say it doesn't matter, anything, whatever and I'd say if you could have any food what would it be -I'll get it for you, whatever you want....you wanted soup cause you were sick and a regular breakfast of bacon and eggs. We drove around for a long while with the kids and Maddie and uncle lu. just laughing and smiling.

It left off you telling me you had to go see your sisters now while I go to work.

I love you dad. Great way to start off my Thursday on a positive note and good vibes.

9/4/14

Losing you

Hearing you say you love me
Seeing people enter the room, hearing you greeting
I thought to myself this can't be it
This can't be the end, can it?
Looking in your eyes, I knew I was losing you
Tears slowly coming from your eyes, you knew too
How do you get comfortable knowing you're going away
How can you be comfortable in so much pain
Moments of watching you make recovery steps gave me so much hope
Moments watching you suffer, hurt me the most
Sleepless nights seeing you unable to eat, unable to speak clear
I was trying to be strong for you, I was trying to hide my fear
But i never felt right to lie, to say I knew we'd be ok
I hoped we would , i prayed for it, I put my trust in faith
I told myself whatever happens that it was meant to be
There's a reason for everything, even if it's hard to see
.....I love you dad
Reliving those last moments haunts me at night
Brings tears to my eyes. there's no comfort for that.... I just wanted to save you; I'll never know why cancer had to take you

Leo's asking about you
Asking when will you come back
Saying he misses his grandpa
There's nothing I can say to that
At the same time I miss you dad
Its very hard to be strong with tear filled eyes

9/2/14

Not enough

there aren't enough words to say how much I miss you, there aren't enough languages to say it in, there aren't enough actions to relieve the pain. Facebook statuses, messages, pictures, posts, videos are all I have left and I am so thankful because some don't have any of that.it brings a little comfort to see posts like this. thank you for your love and words dad, I always wanted to make you proud and take care of you and help you live happy.

8/29/14

Dream

last night you were in my dream, we were getting off a train and you came to help us unpack, you couldn't walk very well and I said dad its ok we got it and you said Caroline I got it...seeing you face, hearing your voice. I loved that but seeing you still suffering, I didn't like that, it's not how I want to remember you and you deserve to be free because after all you are no longer in pain. I miss you

My husband said so that's why you woke up in a good mood today

Yes thank you dad and 9am work schedule

8/26/14

Only 1 you

there is no hug in this world that will ever match yours.
There's no smile that shines as bright and pure.
There's no laugh that sounds the same.
No voice that can imitate.
There's no one who can fill your shoes
No one who can compare or dare to replace you.
So many days I sit in my tears.
Digital frame going while we eat daily pretending your here
I was never ready to accept you would die
I will never be able to say goodbye
I miss you dad

8/4/14

Here

I know I talk about you like your still here,
it's the only way I can smile without tears.
when i stop and put too much thought,
that's when tears start and won't stop.
oldies playing all day remind me of you.
I love and miss you, we all do.

6/28/14

All we wanted

so much bothers me
...those last 2 days you were here, was traumatizing.
all you wanted was to have your spit cup, to use the bathroom, to do the simple things- we take for granted
all I wanted was to take your oxygen mask off, to feed you, to hear you speak, to see you smile and not struggle through it.
All I wanted was to wipe your tears
to let you know that you'll always be ok and mean it, even through my tears and fears.
I know you wanted us to accept what you already had you were ready for peace. That meant I was leaving without my dad.
you were ready for that paradise in heaven you always spoke of
you were surrounded by love.
those days and moments still play in my mind
those moments in my mind still hurt so bad and I still wish I could change time.
As much as I want you back, I am so thankful you're not hurting anymore
as much as I miss you-I know you were strong and happy for so long and couldn't fight it anymore.

I know you were at peace with life and death
You made peace with it, you accepted it.
Losing you has not gotten easier
Missing you feels heavier and heavier.

Your birthday coming up

my brain won't stop trying to prepare for next week, it won't let me not think of it
your birthday July 2 (also the day my bff is scheduled for a c-section).
I always tried to make your birthday special
I always wanted you to feel loved, this will be no different, your day is still special.
you and I always celebrated loved ones who passed
we didn't let nay birthdays go un-noticed whether that person was here physically or in spirit.
A's firework night July 3 you always went with us, 4th of July was one of your favorites
You would dedicate the sky's show to your sister pauly who is in heaven, we could never forget.
it's going to be all so very different without you here
I still need to get my A's shirt with your picture. When I am at the games, I want you right here.

6/23/14

Not long enough

you didn't live in this house with us long enough
I am thankful for those 2 1/2 months.
it was great making you breakfast, lunch, dinner,
it was great seeing you able to relax and use me for whatever.
It was nice being able to help.
it was nice seeing your smile every day and not just on the weekends.
It was so nice and I wish it didn't have to end.
I was looking forward to a new year of holidays in the same house and so much more
Like having you live comfortably and at peace, with all the support.
I know you got that these last few months.
I know we all lose people all the time but it doesn't make missing you any easier,
it doesn't make losing you less painful.
I miss our Walgreens trips, nations breakfast, walks to the gas station,
I miss me telling you that's too much salt or too much junk foods
I miss every little thing.
you living here was not easy.

I had to watch you suffer in pain and discomfort,
I had to hear and see you struggle,
I had to help you get dressed and I loved every moment I got to help you.
I never felt frustrated or like you were bothering me.
I am human, at moments when I felt too busy -I always said to myself "think of how he must feel",
I was grateful to help and I would have done it forever if that meant I could have you here.
I know you knew it was time, you wanted to end the struggle
I am thankful you are no longer in pain or discomfort.
I still wish you would have wanted to accept a living donor route
but you had your beliefs and I had to accept your path chosen.
Thank you for giving me so much just by being you.
I miss you; I love you.

6/17/14

First father's day

this will be the first Father's Day without you dad and my heart hurts so bad I can't even explain the pain and sadness. I can't even explain how great of a man you were and are and will always be. I can't even find all the words to describe how much I miss you. My tears can't express it, I miss you so much, I love you so much and it just hurts so bad and I can't help but want you back.
I had a dream you were here; we were talking. I was so happy to just sit and talk with you and get a hug. You were laying down and I was next to your bed and I got to say happy Father's Day.......
Happy Father's Day dad. I love you past life
It's hard getting up today
I'm finding it hard to say happy Father's Day.
I'm finding it hard to smile,
sad to see all the pictures of people with their dads.
Before you left, I knew how much I loved you and I knew what I had before it was gone,
I knew I didn't want to live a single day without you but even then, I didn't realize how extra hard holidays would be,
I didn't realize how broken id be on a daily basis.
no one can take your place.
I lost you physically but I know you're up there proud of my husband and how much he's changed,

I can't be prouder because his changes now will help him be around longer for the kids.

To my husband thank you. you became a father so young and we have 3 beautiful children and nothing is better than watching them grow up with you in their lives, watching you all play outside and eat together and laugh together. You're a great dad, the best. We love you. Happy Father's Day to the two best dads in the world. I am very blessed and thankful.

Is it mean to say it's hard, to even celebrate and say these things to my husband?

Because when I say he is the best dad-I mean it.

But it also makes me think of my dad and him being the best dad. I mean it.

It was hard for me to say happy Father's Day to my husband. Because I couldn't say it without knowing I don't have my dad hear to say it to him. I couldn't say it with happiness knowing my dad is gone. I couldn't say it without tears.

Grief really hits you in unexpected ways. I feel wrong for how I feel. I feel upset that my hurt is affecting how I treat others. I feel upset that I can't get past my hurt quickly. I am also just accepting it as it comes, as it is. I don't want to pretend it is what it isn't. This is my journey and I am allowing it.

6/15/14

Dream visits

When you visit me in my dreams, I always bring up the funeral or hospital.
I'm very aware it took place and I ask how are you here? then we just go with it as if the funeral and hospital was the real bad dream.
Those dreams feel so real. I can really feel those hugs and hear your voice and then when I wake up-a piece of me goes missing again and I lose what I so badly want to hold on to...
it's just a dream. My camera doesn't work there and reality always comes back to hit me as hard as the day you left.
Thank you for visiting me dad.... I wish you were still here; I love you so much. Father's Day will never be the same. I know you are still with me but I wish you were physically. I want you to know how loved you are and how missed you are and how special you are. I wish all of that could bring you back and keep you here but unfortunately life and death don't work that way. We have to go on and it hurts. its hard. I wish it was different.
I am still so thankful

6/14/14

Leos birthday, my treat

I had a dream of you last night. You were at my bedroom window smiling calling Leo and singing happy birthday. Then i said "dad you made it for Leos birthday" and I pulled you aside saying "I know this is hard to say and I love these moments…with you being sick can we make a bunch of videos of you for the kids with messages for days like today so they never miss out?" we spent the days making videos for them.

Then I woke up….it was a dream but it was so real…. happy birthday Leo, grandpa loves you so much…. it's not the same without you dad…I hope you had a chance to visit Leo last night also…we miss and love you so much

6/2/14

Whose shirt is it

when you passed away, I gave your clothes to family first, Edgardo, uncle Lu, family then friends-people i knew you'd want to help or would appreciate wearing your stuff.
Leo noticed uncle lu in a shirt(Mario one from the kids Mario party) and says to uncle lu: uncle lu why you wearing my grandpas shirt?
uncle lu: because he gave it to me
Leo: no he didn't, that's his shirt
uncle lu: can I have it?
Leo: well he's going to want it back
I am so happy Leo has so many memories of my dad and it also makes me so sad. Leo doesn't understand. I am happy my dad lives on in his memories, pictures, shirts, on other people....
my kids deserve that-they deserve to remember you forever dad because you are and always will be the best dad and grandpa in this whole universe.
we miss and love you-forever and always

5/28/14

The blanket that helps heal

yesterday my niece, my mom, myself and Leo went to the cemetery. I did not tell Leo where we were going. Then a neighbor walked by and asked 'where are you going?" and Leo said loud and proud with excitement "IM GOING TO SEE MY GRANDPA!"
I then felt I had to explain. I tried to prepare him that grandpa won't be there the way he thinks but I couldn't. He would just have to see. He didn't understand why grandpa wasn't there. Leo asked why were we leaving gifts there instead of giving them to him and he keeps asking when are we really going to see grandpa.

I received one of the best gifts yesterday, a huge blanket of a picture of my dad with writing. I cried happy tears. I love it. I know how much my dad loved the one of my grandpa Robert that was made for my grandma and I know he's in heaven so proud someone did this for me. but now Leo and iris want the blanket all for them, they love it, the want to sleep with it and won't stop talking about it.... I am going to have to make them their own because this one is mine lol

5/27/14

Help those in need

on the way to the cemetery we saw a man sitting outside with an oxygen tank trying to collect money.
when I was younger, I was always quick to reach in my pocket to help anyone who asked, homeless or not.
it was when I was younger that I always wanted to do more. To give food, clothes, blankets-whatever people needed.
It was when I was younger that I had several moments when people were not happy with food, they would get mad. That is when I learned on a different level that some people are addicts. I then wasn't so quick to reach in my pockets to give money because I didn't want to help people with their bad habits. I wanted to help people in need of things many of us take for granted.
My dad would give anyone change who needed it. I would question him why, especially when he would say "I can tell that person is going to get a beer" My dad would say who are we to judge? I use to be that person and many people helped me in my time of need" He would tell me he knows how it feels to be an addict, to feel low, to feel in need, to be out on the streets. He would explain to me everyone has their own journey and it's not our job to judge.

I still prefer to give food but I will give the change I have. My dad chose to get clean and sober and change his life for me which lead him to a better life with family, himself and then he was blessed with grandkids "I get to start over with them"

My dad ended up taking classes to be a counselor to help people. unfortunately, upon graduation was around the time he got sick and was battling his fight with cancer. He didn't get to live the dream exactly how he wanted but that didn't mean he didn't try to help people. He would share his spiritual views, his faith, his education and most importantly his experiences with anyone he felt called to.

Thank you dad for always giving, always being caring, always seeing the other side, never forgetting where you came from-never ashamed of your past or scars or everyday challenges. Thank you for being so honest and open and helpful. I love you dad

1/22/17

I celebrate you

Missing you so much
Wish I could get your hug
You live in all of our smiles
Athena with your chin and Leo with your style
Father's Day isn't the same without you
But I celebrate the men in my life who care for me like dads do
I celebrate you , there's no one the same
I celebrate my husband- you two were similar in ways
Thank you for giving me so much to miss
Thank you for the memories and the dream visits ♡

6/20/20

It's Ok

I want you to know its ok.
its ok if you no longer want to fight this fight.
its ok if you want to move on from this life.
I will be ok, you don't have to stay for me.
I will be ok, you don't have to continue suffering.
I want you to know its ok.
if you still want to fight, I will be your warrior.
if you still want this life here, say no more.
I want you to know its ok.
if your tired and need rest, please lay.
if your feeling up to getting up I will not stand in your way.
I won't tell you to rest if you want to walk.
I won't tell you to walk if you want to lay.
however you feel, its ok.
we know your battle but we can't feel your pain.
we know heartache but it's not the same.
you are the true warrior every single day.
you are the true fighter, fighting always.
your body is fighting even when its sleeping.
your body is true strength even as its weakening.
your eyes say what your words don't.
your words say what you fear you one day wont.

I want you to know its ok.
I am here to make sure you feel your best every day.
its ok to sit, its ok to not do all you use to.
its ok to close your eyes, its ok to cry too.
its ok to not be ok.
its ok to say the things I don't want to hear you say.
we all know we all will go.
we all know but we still don't know.
doctors put a timeframe on your life.
and although this has been said, there's no planning for that time.
its ok to live as if days aren't numbered.
its ok to live as if there will be no tomorrow.
only you know how you feel.
what's on your mind and in your heart. your own real.
I would keep you here forever if I could.
please don't base your journey on my idea of good.
its ok if you are ready to let this go
you didn't choose this battle but you've endured this road.
road to recovery doesn't always happen
sometimes the destination is not what we would have chosen.
sometimes we are faced to make peace with death
to accept the fact that -that's what's left.
and it has to be ok.

because when you've tried everything to avoid the inevitable, it doesn't always go your way

7/8/17

Carolina Ayala

The hardest thing I had to do

The hardest thing I've ever had to do was watch you slip away
to watch you in pain and know I couldn't make it go away.
the hardest thing I've ever had to do was know I was losing you
but I had to live life happy to have the days I had left with you.
to know the years were limited but the day was unknown
knowing you wanted your life to run its course but you also wanted to hold on.
it was not easy watching you have cancer
all those medicines, radiations and procedures.
it's the hardest thing to accept you're going to lose someone you love
to know life will never be the same , to know your battle can't be won.
it's the hardest thing ever to talk about death like it's all a part of the plan
to make funeral plans like it won't break me as I stand.
as I stand without you beside me
as life goes on without you beside me.
cancer makes you physically weak but it gives you

Healing While Hurting

strength you never knew you had
it makes life worth living , while feeling so bad.
you have been gone a few years now and it still feels like yesterday
you were ready to let go, I wanted to tell you stay.
but instead I accepted you were ready and I said it was ok
"what's meant to be will be"-doesn't take the pain away.
no words make it better, no gifts replace what was
but you are no longer in pain -you suffered more than too much.
I have to find peace in the way your face changed,
when you closed your eyes that last time and I felt you slip away.
all the pain left your face, I hope you found peace
I fear how can you, knowing you truly didn't want to leave.
selfish me wanted you to keep fighting
but the other part of me knew that was not living, it just wasn't dying.
and there is a difference
I still wish it was different.
love you forever and always, always and forever

7/8/17

Peaceful soul

I just want your soul to be at peace...
and mine as well
after over 5 years of you being gone-today was the first day of that.
I gave myself permission and saw it through.
it was my gift to you - because I know you cannot be at peace if I am not at peace
and nothing hurts me more than to think you are hurt -especially because of me
and I've always felt that way and still it never mattered, until today.
today/yesterday it mattered differently.
today we celebrated differently and everything happened so perfectly
we just went with the flow
and in doing so we received blessings on blessings from morning till night.
and it all gives me even more peace that today's shift was the right shift .
for you, for me, for all of us missing and loving you.
I saw a difference in the kids too.
it was beautiful.
we love you dad.

7/2/19

I can hear you, I can feel you

I wouldn't have left you if I knew leaving you would
mean you would lose yourself
you were my favorite person
I left because I know you were strong enough to let me go
I know you knew it was my time to go
you know I would have stayed if I could hold on longer
you know I wouldn't have left if I had the choice of forever
I know you are strong, I know you are strong
I knew leaving would hurt
I didn't think you'd lose the parts of you I loved so much
I knew leaving you wasn't what I wanted
you are not lost, you just aren't healing
like me you are stubborn and hurting
you are scared to move on and lose what's left of me
I need you to move on so I can move on and I can be
happy with you being happy
I need you to heal
I am healed
you can never forget me, I am not worried about that
I am you, you are me, the kids have me forever attached
but it is ok to heal
I need you to heal
we both need to move on

I know the hurt is strong
I miss you too
I love you too
but its ok to heal. that doesn't mean love is gone
its ok to heal, that is never wrong
please find peace
I am at peace
………...hey dad,
here I am talking to you again, talking with you again…. hearing you again.
I just wish I could hug you again and have you here again.

5/25/19

They say time heals

I don't know when or if I'll ever be able to let you go
I'm not sure I can ever heal
I know you never would like to see me sad
And it probably hurts you more because you aren't here.
You aren't here to help cheer me up
And cancer is the reason for the pain
You probably feel responsible
But you are not to blame.
I'm sorry I'm still so sad
But I miss you so much, love you dad.
I know you are with grandpa Robert and I thank you for putting him in my life when you did
I'm thankful to still have grandma Katie and all of my cousins
I know you are with uncle Larry, both sharing the humor and laughing away
I hope you see my grandma Madeleine and fill her in on missed days.
Please keep my aunt Denise company , even though I know my cousin Wayne is by her side
I know you're eating good with Jossie, like we always did back in time.
My uncle john joined you all , somewhat recently

I know you guys are probably good friends up there
-both role models the world needs.
I'm sure you are like a little boy up there- getting to be with your mom
And you've got your sister Pauly- heaven is starting to sound real good.
So many people I love , no longer here
So many people I miss, makes it harder here.
So many guardian angels to keep me safe
I miss you more than ever but I hope I have a long time before I add my name.
Rest in Peace loved ones.
I know Chata, your godmother and so many more of your loved ones are living it up with you in the next life.
That brings me peace.
Even though I feel so incomplete.
They say time heals.
.... they say time heals

5/14/19

Birthday number 3

Birthday number 3
Without you here physically
Countless times I still cry
Like a child I still ask why
I still find myself saying I can't believe your gone
I still find myself feeling like you're not gone
I miss seeing your face, seeing your smile, receiving your hugs
I miss having you here, having you near, I miss my father's love
You were too young to go but cancer cares not about age
You were deserving of second chance being clean and sober for over a decade
And you had your second chance
And had to pay for your past
I'm so sorry I couldn't save you
I'm so sorry a huge piece of me left with you
Without you I'll never be who I used to be
Without you days just can't mean what they used to mean
Memories live on
Sadness lives on
Gratitude outweighs it all

Love outweighs it all
Happy birthday dad.... it's hitting me hard. I've been holding myself together pretty well for awile until now

7/2/16

I look at all your pictures-your smile-your spirit-your soul. I don't see someone who can be defeated by any illness. living with you I was able to let you rest better and be able to depend a little on me, lean on me. I loved every second dad, even the hard ones. You were never trouble. I hated being busy with work and other duties but I loved sitting with you watching tv, holding you, sharing cries, sharing stories and conversations. You loved your new phone and going on fb and taking new profile pictures, lying in bed on your laptop. Oh, how I miss you so much, everything about you. Your smell still lingers in the room. Your face in my mind. Your love in my heart. You live through me and the kids. some moments I feel I should have made you hold on but, in many thoughts, I know I did right by respecting your wishes to let go. I couldn't make you hold on. I couldn't put that extra stress and pain on you. I couldn't change what was real. I know you were at peace because you always were with me. you had all loved ones and the kids; you have everyone who mattered most and kept you alive and healthy. we will all forever keep you living on here. I can still feel your touch and hear your voice. I never want those reminders. I never want those memories to leave me. I have always been proud of you. I will forever be proud of you and try to continue to make you proud of me.

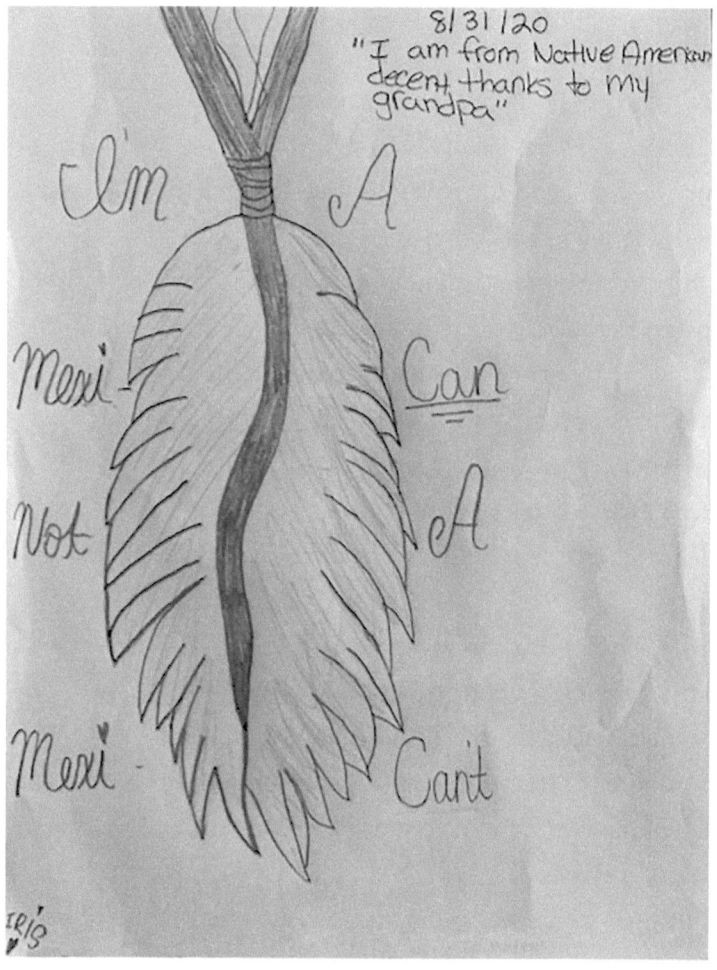

Out Loud

I am not sure I have ever read these words out loud
before
it is different for sure.
but, I wanted to hear me
I wanted to imagine a reader reading.
The tears fall so heavily
my nose got too stuffy, sometimes it was hard to speak.
will the readers feel me?
will I reach others and help them allow their feelings?
no one's journey is the same
we share ourselves, not because we are the same.
we share because others can relate
we share to help others feel brave and safe.
we share so others know "you are not alone"
I share because it helps me heal and it is good for my
soul.
I feel like I don't know where to start
and I don't know how to end
sometimes I debate if I know what I am doing
sometimes I question why I started.
I have always wanted to write a book, I have so many
ideas and drafts
but this one called to me and it was never one I had
planned.

hey dad, I love you.

always and forever,

forever and always

it still feels unreal and scary to put out there, what I am doing

I feel like I shouldn't talk until the goal is complete and the dream isn't just dreaming.

I know you will help me through this, you have all this time

I know it will all come together, but it's hard to imagine with so much on my mind

how can I fit so much into 1 book?

maybe it's just the first of more to come, maybe it will be enough, just 1 tiny book.

10/4/20

Carolina M-g Ayala-Velasquez

June 29, 2019 ·
you have been on my mind a lot. A lot a lot, lately.
I am really working on fixing me, the part of me that died with you.
I know the soul doesn't die and you aren't gone but yet a piece of me has been forever gone and I know that's not what you would want.
I am spending your birthday coming up in full celebration, that is my declaration-my promise to you-I give myself permission for that. It does not mean no tears; it just means no depression this time. This time I will simply celebrate your life. I will not sulk.
I love you dad.

Carolina M-g Ayala-Velasquez

April 27, 2019 ·

I remember someone saying I have to stop crying for my dad because it means I'm not letting him move on. I still cry often. I still remember seeing you take your last breath and wishing I did things different to keep you longer even though it wasn't my decision to make. I still feel so sad knowing you knew you were going to die and that you had to live with being strong for us, smiling with us, you had to live with not wanting to leave us but also wanting to rest. I was so emotional while pregnant with Athena knowing she would never physically meet and know you-and then she was a miracle baby and born with your chin-the only one. that's not just coincidence. she is 1 and she holds your buttons and just stares at you like she knows you. maybe she does. the kids still talk about you often. they miss you as much as I do at times, they cry like I do-they enjoy videos and get sad at them as well. we are always reminded of memories with you. I hear your voice in my head often as things happen. I hear your voice; I remember your ways. we are so much alike and yet so different. when you left I really lost me, things changed. I lost me and it hasn't always been a good thing and I haven't yet found my way back to the me I was before. back to the daughter you loved so much. I have changed. and it has been hard. I was baptized a few years ago and in connection more than ever spiritually and yet was faced with the biggest challenges and changes more than ever and I have been conflicted more than ever. it has been a crazy journey. I am very slowly finding my way back. it's been over 5 years and I am just barley starting to make my way back to me. life is the hardest this year in many ways and blessings are strong but it's been hard and now I am re-finding who I am and who I am meant to be. I love and miss you dad

Thankful
(what has helped me through. What continues to help me heal. How I honor my dad. How my family celebrates his life)

This will look different for everyone.
For me I have some things that helped me at different times during this process of grieving. What helps me through and how we honor my dad many times goes hand in hand. Healing hurts. Healing can also feel so peaceful, when it really starts coming to be what its meant to be. I believe every part of the process (whatever that feels and looks like for you), is what it's meant to be and serves a purpose.

-crying. Allowing myself that time and space to feel whatever is real.
-Writing poetry
-Writing to my dad on Facebook
-Writing out my thoughts and feelings
-Putting a box away of some of his belongings I knew I wanted to hold on to
-For the Vigil and Funeral, I had shirts made of my dad for people to have and wear and keep. I also allowed anyone to pitch in money who could for them. I put my favorite picture of him smiling with a phrase he would say all the time on the back "Don't thank me, Thank GOD."

-I bought a digital frame, specifically for picture memories of my dad to play at the vigil and to keep at home

-I made a banner at Walgreens to hang at the reception and to keep at home. To honor his time in the marines. He was proud of that.

-I made two collage poster boards for the vigil and funeral. I let two of my dad's siblings each take one home.

-My husband got me a locket to put my dads' picture in it, necklace.

-I bought bears for the kids that have hearts inside. Those hearts hold recorded messages. My dads voice from old videos I had (personal recordable plush)

-I bought the kids in memory bears that came with a poem and had space to put a picture of them in it (whispers from heaven)

-I bought two books "where is grandpa?" By Olan Menetta and "When someone you love has cancer": a guide to help kids cope By Elf help books for kids

-while in reno I bought a bracelet that I got to put my dad's picture and my own words on

-I had several shirts made just for me of pictures/quotes from my dad (some I used his real Facebook posts and had them put on the picture shirt) I would wear different shirts for different occasions. (Thank you Joe Ortega)

-My sister Nicole made me a sweater that had a picture of my dad and a Facebook quote of his

-I made blankets for the kids from Walgreens of collage of pictures

-A family member made me a woven blanket of my dad with a message that we keep on my bed and hang for every special occasion. It is life size (Thank you Pat and uncle Rudy)

-someone made me a picture poem frame (Thank you to my cousin Elise)

-I made two different kinds of buttons of my dad to pass out to people. It was cheaper than the shirts and easier to have on hand for special moments

--When it comes to any special day for us, we spray my dad's cologne. I bought a back up one so we can save his personal one for the extra special days.

-we hang a blanket of him

-we play digital frame

-sometimes we visit the cemetery

-the digital frame of his pictures

-we speak about him

-we wear shirts or buttons in memory of him

-We still celebrate his birthday and passing with food he enjoyed, people who join.

-sometimes I ask the kids how they would like to celebrate

-for the funeral we released doves,
it was important for me to include people during this time (in picking his music, in giving pictures, in having enough favors, asking people to speak, having someone sing)
-At the funeral Adrianna Kramer sang Hero by Mariah Carey.
"I can't ever watch it without balling my eyes out
I sang this song at an elementary event because I loved this song and my dad wanted me to sing
its only right it was sung at his funeral....not by me but by someone very talented who also meant a lot to him
HERO-Mariah Carey
my dad, my hero"
-as the kids are older, I have passed on some of his jewelry and items
-some one made me CDs of pictures and songs (Thank you Raymond Corral)
-writing this book has helped me heal and I plan to write another of the happier times, a keepsake for my family of memories
-sometimes I wear shirts that used to be my dad's (that now belong to my husband)
-I remember my dad's saying "don't thank me, thank GOD"
-loved ones writing posts to him, to me- helps me

-I made a "to remember Juan Ayala" group where people can post and connect
-I left his Facebook open
- I sold his car as fast as I could, I gave away his clothes to family and people in need
- We have an altar at home. Some call it an Ofrenda. It is a space we have set up to honor loved ones who have passed away.
-I take days off of work like the day of his birthday or the date of his passing. When my dad passed away, I took a couple of weeks off of work. I learned about bereavement time off and used that.
-as time has passed, I have still come across very painful moments. Like getting married in church and not having my dad to walk me or be there. However, I was so thankful he was there when I got married in 2010.
The birth of my last child Athena was a new first without him. She is the first of his grandchildren who will never have met him. But yet she knows him, she points to his picture and says grandpa. She knew him before we ever told her who he is. She pointed to the ceiling and said "bye grandpa when she was even younger. She is only 2 ½ now.
When I got baptized, my dad was not here for that. But it was something we had talked about a lot and I could feel his presence with me.

Writing this book, I wish he was alive to know it but obviously then it would never be what it is.

As loved, one's lost their dads, I feel so deeply connected because of my experience. It takes me back every time and I have to process the feelings.

It is still hard for me to know how to show up for others when they are dealing with loss. Anytime someone loses someone, I don't know how to help. It is hard to know what to say or do.

With each painful challenge, there is a positive to it. I try to remind myself of that. I try to allow myself to feel whatever is present and be ok with what is-while also holding gratitude and positivity.

-being myself, being true to me and my feelings, my thoughts, my healing, my truths, my journey- has helped me come this far

And I hope it helps anyone reading to feel safe to be themselves and all the layers to themselves

Grateful
(What I wish I knew. What I learned along the way)

Some things I wish I knew and still want to do

-I wish I knew what he wanted: to be cremated or buried
There are some things I still want to do: like go fishing with the boys/family-because that's an experience he wanted to do

I want to participate in more relays for life to support cancer survivors and honor his journey with cancer and his life

I want to one day make our own altar at the day of the dead festival in Oakland in honor of him and my loved ones who have passed away

-I still hope to get to know more of my dads' side of the family.

-I still want to write more books about my dad. Happier times of his life, lessons he taught me, a keepsake for the family of photos and quotes and stories

I learned a lot about myself

-I learned how expensive funerals are. I learned how expensive death is, financially.
It is also expensive physically, emotionally, mentally, spiritually.
-I met some of my family I didn't know
-My husband and I are working with our moms to fill out books, that they can leave for the kids and family one day
- I learned the importance of life insurance
-I wish I took more videos of my dad and time with him
- I learned about how my dad's time in the marines really ended up helping us during the funeral and added extra support/celebration
-writing an obituary taught me about my dad and his family-things I didn't know
-I have learned that it is ok to not be ok

People will understand what you share. People will support if you reach out or allow them. I am not usually someone who takes support willingly but this phase of my life taught me to be open to it and embrace it with open arms. Part of my thoughts around that were that others were grieving too and maybe that was their way of making peace with the hurt.

I had to also allow myself to be ok with being ok. After so long of not being ok- sometimes it didn't feel right to feel better. When I would write "I didn't cry today" I would feel a sense of guilt. This past year I reached a point where I didn't cry on his 6-year anniversary and I reached a point that it felt good. No guilt, no tears. The pain still was there but it wasn't felt like before and I was finally ok with that. I was ok with the hurt that was still present and I was ok with the healing. I always have known my dad wouldn't want me to be sad, but that didn't help me not be sad. I had to deal with the feelings. I had to feel the feelings.

Blessed (Thank you)

*Thank you for supporting me by reading this book. Thank you for owning it, for keeping my dad alive, for sharing my journey, for taking the time.

* Thank you, dad, for continuing to inspire and help me grow, because even though you're in heaven-I am constantly trying to make you proud, I am always learning from you and I carry you with me everywhere I go and with all I do.

*Thank you to my children and my husband for believing in me and supporting me.

Angel, Iris, Leo and Athena, for keeping your grandpa's legacy alive through you all.

Thank you, mom, for life. (Your book is coming next mom "ratchet grandma")

To all of my family who ride this journey with me, I know I am never alone.

*Thank you to my husband. For sticking by me through all of my stages of grief and healing. For allowing my feelings to be what they are and without judgment. For pushing me when I needed it. For holding me when I needed it. For helping honor my dad in the ways that brought me peace.

*Thank you to all of my friends and family who were by my side those final days in the hospital, who helped me with planning arrangements after, who attended the vigil and funeral, who put on a shirt or button in honor of my dad, who visit the cemetery, who send their love, who pray for him or us, who share pictures and stories, anyone who has ever messaged or wrote me or wrote about my dad in anyway, anyone who wished they could have been there & wanted to be there, anyone who has ever had good intentions when it comes to my father, me and my family-I appreciate you all.

I wish I could thank every single person by name. Please know you mean so much to me and I hope you feel honored, heard, seen and loved. (Becky for your poems, decorating the tables at the ceremony, Sonya for your constant love and gifts out of this world)

*My Padilla family- I am so thankful my dad kept us in connection and involved.

*Anyone who helps keep his memory alive in any way, anyone who celebrates his life in anyway, Desirae for the pamphlets.

*Thank you Julie Lieberman Neale for your continuous support, connections, opportunities, love and guidance.

*Tiny book course for helping me with making this dream a reality with your course you offer. To become an author and to honor my father in this way.

*Thank you, Barbara Schmidt, for bringing poetry into my life in the 4th grade and continuing to remain in my life with your love and support. So happy you are in remission.
*Thank you to my cousin Maddie for taking me to Alameda hospital, for rushing me to Fremont, for sleeping with me in the hospital and never leaving me, for getting the kids so they could be there to say goodbye.
*Thank you, Heidi and Sharon, for reading my rough draft and giving me your feedback before I released this to the world.
*Thank you to myself. For being true to me, for being brave and for making it happen.
*My dad would thank you all. He was so happy to see everyone that last day. Listening to everyone's words gave him happiness and ease. I can't thank everyone enough for helping me support his last wish that day. I know he is thankful for this book, to touch and help more lives. His gifts continue to give.
*To My Altamirano family-I love you and am always here for you.
(Rest in Peace Gabriel Altamirano)
I can't say I know how you feel
I can't tell you how to heal.
yes it's now true, we both lost our dads
but our stories couldn't be more different.
on some level I know your pain

Healing While Hurting

but it will never be the same.
I wish I could take your hurt away
but from my experience, it never goes away.
from my experience there is nothing anyone can do
I know you are hurting-all I can do is be here for you.
I am here to listen, I am here for a hug
I am here to hold you, I am here to share love.
I am here and can share pain with you
I can share healing too.
I can share my journey with you
but I can never tell you what will be true.
my experiences are only mine
I can never know your pain, I can never know it just because I know mine.
I can maybe say we share similarities
I can maybe share some things that helped me.
but what worked for me may not work for you
what helped me may not be what helps you.
on a human level, on empathy
I can relate to you and you can relate to me.
I see you struggling to cope and I know I have been there
heck, sometimes I'm still there.
but that may not be your story in some years, or maybe it will
I can't say I know how you feel, I can't tell you I know how you will heal.

I can share my journey and hope it helps
I can share and it may not help.
my process is just mine
I feel so strong for your loss, because of what I felt with mine.
I feel so strong because of the love I have for you
because of my experiences with who's now gone too.
but I can never be in your shoes
I can never feel how you do.
all I can do is pray for you
all I can do is be here for you.
to my Altamirano family. sending you love. you guys stay on my mind and heart and I'm praying for you through the days for whatever you may be going through.
However, this part of life and death is affecting you. here if you need me, however I can be. My condolences.

9/12/20

*To my mother-in-law who continues to fight on her cancer journey-we love you and continue to thank you for brining GOD into our lives even more. Thank you, GOD, for her.

Re-living it all through this book

Re-living some of these posts, some of these writings,
some of these readings and poems
I put on some helping music, some healing sounds of
Jhene to get me through and help me
I did not realize…how much work this would be
or maybe I did, maybe that's why I have been
procrastinating
This tiny book can only be as perfect as it can be
it could never be everything
but dad this is speaking to me
this is my journey
healing while hurting
you have always been with me
yes, even as you left me
you never left me
it's taken me some time to get to this place I am at right
now sitting here
it's taken me years and it will take me more years
I have a month to get this done
so that this book can be in the hands of me and loved
ones
this book to honor you
the man I know, not just who people knew
I am writing this book because you live on

I am writing this book because my healing no longer feels wrong
this is a forever thing
going through the pain while healing
Even though I have so much written, this is going to take some time
time to get it right
to figure each peace out
but the word is out
I am doing this
I have claimed it
it is happening
and I hope you are proud of me
man, these tears never seem to stop, even as time goes on, I can feel those feelings from years ago as if it was right now
I am for certain, this will just be book 1..........
 love you dad
always and forever
forever and always
I finally put in time today, to really take it beyond the journal and posts
I finally put in time today, to type it up and get more clear on structure
making my vision real
and I am feeling all of the feels

I am doing this for me
I am doing this for my family
I am doing this for anyone who has lost someone
anyone who is healing while hurting, anyone who cancer
has somehow touched
to anyone who has felt grief
to anyone who loves poetry
for anyone who can use some reflection
to anyone, for unknown reasons
......it's coming along
my first tiny book.....
send all the good vibes this way

10/21/20

* Everything written in this is what keeps me going.

I wrote this tiny book, a book of poetry and reflections. I did this for me, because it called for me, because it is for my healing, because it is for my family, because it is to honor my dad, and because I have always wanted to write a book.

To anyone who has ever liked a post, commented, messaged me because they were touched in any way-thank you.

You let me know that people beyond myself and family could be touched by my words and experiences. This pain and healing is not just mine and I am never alone. I hope you don't feel alone in your journey.

Carolina M-g Ayala-Velasquez

April 23 ·

Athena just laid down and pointed at the Ceiling "grandpa"
I was caught by surprise and took a moment and then I said "you see grandpa?"
She says "nope!... he left.... bye bye grandpa"
I am feeling so many feelings right now ♡😲♡
She's never physically met her grandpa. She has his chin. She seems to know who he is.

Carolina M-g Ayala-Velasquez

March 7 ·

Athena keeps saying "grandpa coming "

Carolina M-g Ayala-Velasquez

January 25 ·

Athena just asked for the movie coco and said "grandpa" then pointed to my dads blanket.
She loves the movie coco and has been asking for it daily. But the way it just went- that gave me chills

Carolina M-g Ayala-Velasquez

June 15, 2018 ·

Athena is 3 months old today. My heart hurts constantly knowing she will never meet my dad; she will know of him from stories and pictures but will never meet him the way iris angel and Leo were able to. Athena has probably met his during and knows his unconditional love. She shares my middle name of Guadalupe given to me by my dad. Athena your grandpa loves you, he would have spoiled you just like the rest. ♡

About the author

Carolina Ayala (who many also know as Lena) is a mother to four children: Angel, Iris, Leonardo and Athena. She is the wife to Edgardo Velasquez. She has lived most of her life in Alameda, CA. Over the last 7 years, she has been a teacher. She has taught infant care, toddler care and pre-school. She has also taught high-school (as a substitute and as a child development after-school teacher). Being a mother, wife, and teacher have always been her passion- so has writing. Growing up, music, writing, reflecting, poetry and gratitude got her through the challenging and good days. She has always been a writer, although this is her first book – it will probably not be her last.

I think there is something very powerful about showing up as you are; about being unpolished, unrehearsed and real. I think honesty creates opportunity for release and healing; and it also creates the space to make genuine connections. I often downplay all I am and what I am doing but now I claim the beauty and power. I did not just write a tiny book or share my diary with the world. I wrote a book! I wrote about what matters to me, and I am putting it into the world so that it can matter to anyone else. Maybe you only connect with the title; maybe you read every page and only enjoy the last. Maybe it's not your type of book. I feel and hope that no-matter what you get from even looking this way; you will get what serves you.

www.ingramcontent.com/pod-product-compliance
Lightning Source LLC
Chambersburg PA
CBHW021440070526
44577CB00002B/229